Communication of Politics: Cross-Cultural Theory Building in the Practice of Public Relations and Political Marketing

Communication of Politics: Cross-Cultural Theory Building in the Practice of Public Relations and Political Marketing has been co-published simultaneously as *Journal of Political Marketing,* Volume 1, Numbers 2/3 2002.

Indexing, Abstracting & Website/Internet Coverage

This section provides you with a list of major indexing & abstracting services. That is to say, each service began covering this periodical during the year noted in the right column. Most Websites which are listed below have indicated that they will either post, disseminate, compile, archive, cite or alert their own Website users with research-based content from this work. (This list is as current as the copyright date of this publication.)

*Special Bibliographic Notes related to special journal issues
(separates) and indexing/abstracting:*

- indexing/abstracting services in this list will also cover material in any "separate" that is co-published simultaneously with Haworth's special thematic journal issue or DocuSerial. Indexing/abstracting usually covers material at the article/chapter level.
- monographic co-editions are intended for either non-subscribers or libraries which intend to purchase a second copy for their circulating collections.
- monographic co-editions are reported to all jobbers/wholesalers/approval plans. The source journal is listed as the "series" to assist the prevention of duplicate purchasing in the same manner utilized for books-in-series.
- to facilitate user/access services all indexing/abstracting services are encouraged to utilize the co-indexing entry note indicated at the bottom of the first page of each article/chapter/contribution.
- this is intended to assist a library user of any reference tool (whether print, electronic, online, or CD-ROM) to locate the monographic version if the library has purchased this version but not a subscription to the source journal.
- individual articles/chapters in any Haworth publication are also available through the Haworth Document Delivery Service (HDDS).

Communication of Politics: Cross-Cultural Theory Building in the Practice of Public Relations and Political Marketing

Bruce I. Newman, PhD
Dejan Verčič, PhD
Editors

Communication of Politics: Cross-Cultural Theory Building in the Practice of Public Relations and Political Marketing has been co-published simultaneously as *Journal of Political Marketing,* Volume 1, Numbers 2/3 2002.

Routledge
Taylor & Francis Group
NEW YORK AND LONDON

First Published by

Harrington Park Press®, an imprint of The Haworth Press, Inc., 10 Alice Street, Binghamton, NY 13904-1580.

Transferred to Digital Printing 2010 by Routledge
270 Madison Ave, New York NY 10016
2 Park Square, Milton Park, Abingdon, Oxon, OX14 4RN

Communication of Politics: Cross-Cultural Theory Building in the Practice of Public Relations and Political Marketing has been co-published simultaneously as *Journal of Political Marketing*™, Volume 1, Numbers 2/3 2002.

Cover design by Marylouise Doyle

Library of Congress Cataloging-in-Publication Data

Communication of politics : cross-cultural theory building in the practice of public relations and political marketing / Bruce I. Newman, Dejan Vercic, editors.
     p. cm.
Published also as v. 1, no. 2/3, 2002, of the Journal of political marketing.
     ISBN 0-7890-2158-7 (case : alk. paper) – ISBN 0-7890-2159-5 (soft : alk. paper)
1. Communication in politics–United States. 2. Communication in politics–Great Britain. 3. Communication in politics–Slovenia. 4. Campaign management–United States. 5. Campaign management–Great Britain. 6. Campaign management–Slovenia. I. Newman, Bruce I. II. Veréciéc, Dejan.
     JA85.2.U6C65 2003
     324.7'3–dc21

                                        2003002282

Communication of Politics: Cross-Cultural Theory Building in the Practice of Public Relations and Political Marketing

CONTENTS

ABOUT THE EDITORS

Bruce I. Newman, PhD, is currently Professor of Marketing at DePaul University, and Visiting Scholar at the Institute of Governmental Studies at the University of California-Berkeley. He is one of the leading experts in the world on the subject of Political Marketing. He combines an expertise in marketing and politics with his knowledge of consumer psychology and statistical applications. He has published seven books and numerous articles on the subjects of political marketing and consumer psychology. Bruce's publications have appeared in both scholarly journals and popular press.

Prior to coming to DePaul University in 1987, he was on the faculty of Baruch College, City University of New York, and the University of Wisconsin-Milwaukee. He was also Visiting Professor at Trinity College in Dublin, Ireland, and a visiting scholar at F.M.D. Research Institute in Oslo, Norway. He received his B.S., M.B.A. and Ph.D. (in 1981) in marketing from the University of Illinois at Champaign-Urbana.

Professor Newman has published extensively in the field of political marketing. He is the author of *The Marketing of the President: Political Marketing as Campaign Strategy*, published in 1994. This book was translated into Korean in 2000 and into Hungarian in 1999. He is the co-author of *A Theory of Political Choice Behavior*, published in 1987; and *Political Marketing: Readings and Annotated Bibliography*, published in 1985.

Professor Newman's most recent book on politics, *The Mass Marketing of Politics: Democracy in an Age of Manufactured Images*, was published in 1999. This book was translated into Hungarian by Bagolyvar Publishing Co. in 1999. He is also the editor of *Handbook of Political Marketing*, published in 1999. This is the first handbook in the field and includes original contributions on the role of marketing in politics from 56 authors, including politicians, consultants, scholars, pollsters and other experts from nine different countries.

Dr. Newman has also published extensively in the field of consumer psychology, and is the co-author of a marketing textbook *Customer Be-*

havior: Consumer Behavior and Beyond, published in 1998; and *Consumption Values and Market Choices: Theory and Applications*, published in 1991. Dr. Newman sits on the editorial boards of several academic journals. Bruce is also a frequent contributor to mass media, with Op-Ed pieces appearing in *The Christian Science Monitor*, *The Sunday Telegraph*, and *The Chicago Tribune*. He has appeared on several nationally syndicated talk shows in both the United States and Britain, and is a regular guest on talk shows in Chicago.

Dr. Newman has lectured to numerous professional groups around the world on the topic of political marketing. Bruce is represented by the Authors Unlimited Lecture Bureau, located in New York City.

He is member of Phi Kappa Phi (and past President), Beta Gamma Sigma, and Sigma Iota Epsilon. Bruce is listed in Strathmore's Who's Who, Who's Who in Advertising, Who's Who of Young Professionals, and Who's Who in Media and Communications. In 1993, Dr. Newman received the Ehrenring (Ring of Honor) from the Austrian Advertising Research Association in Vienna for his research in political marketing. He is the first American recipient of this award in the 30 years it has been awarded.

Dejan Verčič, PhD, is a founding partner in Pristop Communications, a communication management consultancy based in Ljubljana, Slovenia, and Assistant Professor for Public Relations and Communication Management at the University of Ljubljana. Among his clients are governments, domestic and international corporations, and associations. From 1991-1993 he led the foundation of the Slovenian News Agency–STA. He holds a PhD from the London School of Economics.

In 2000 he received a special award by the Public Relations Society of Slovenia for his contributions to the development of public relations practice and research, and in 2001 he was awarded the Alan Campbell-Johnson Medal for outstanding service to international public relations by the UK Institute of Public Relations.

Since 1994 he annually has organized the Lake Bled International Public Relations Research Symposia and he is active in the European Public

Relations Body of Knowledge project. Recent publications include an article 'On the definition of public relations: a European view', *Public Relations Review 27* (2001): 373-387, and a book on *Perspectives on Public Relations Research* (Routledge, 2000).

Dr. Verčič is president-elect of Euprera–The European Public Relations Education and Research Association for 2003.

EDITORIAL

The Merging
of Public Relations and Political Marketing

Political marketing and public relations are two disciplines that have found a home in the field of politics. For many years now, politicians around the world have been advised by professionals in the field of public relations. Since Ronald Reagan was Governor in California, he had been receiving advice from Michael Deaver, a public relations genius who helped shape and sell Reagan's image to the American people by literally wrapping him in the American flag in an attempt to position him as an American hero and patriot (Newman, 1994). Successive presidents since Reagan have all relied on the same kind of public relations advice, including former President Bush, former President Clinton and

[Haworth co-indexing entry note]: "The Merging of Public Relations and Political Marketing." Newman, Bruce I., and Dejan Verčič. Co-published simultaneously in *Journal of Political Marketing* (The Haworth Political Press, an imprint of The Haworth Press, Inc.) Vol. 1, No. 2/3, 2002, pp. 1-7; and: *Communication of Politics: Cross-Cultural Theory Building in the Practice of Public Relations and Political Marketing* (eds: Bruce I. Newman, and Dejan Verčič) The Haworth Political Press, an imprint of The Haworth Press, Inc., 2002, pp. 1-7. Single or multiple copies of this article are available for a fee from The Haworth Document Delivery Service [1-800-HAWORTH, 9:00 a.m. - 5:00 p.m. (EST). E-mail address: getinfo@haworthpressinc.com].

10.1300/J199v01n02_01

President Bush in 2000. Along with public relations advisors, more recently, candidates for all levels of office around the world are also relying on political marketing advisors who use their marketing research skills to generate databases to segment and target appeals to voter groups (Newman, 1999a, 1999b). So what are the common characteristics of both disciplines that help politicians to campaign successfully?

Public relations and political marketing have many common features:

- Both have a focal client (an individual or organization).
- Both relate to one or more groups of people ("publics" in the language of public relations and "markets" in the language of political marketing).
- Both develop around issues (that interest "publics" or "markets").
- Both are (at least normatively) research driven.
- Both (are supposed to) deliver added value to a focal client (who is better off by using them).
- Both emerged as professions through the 20th century.
- Both are growing fast in numbers of people employed and in their structural and geographic spread.
- Both are gaining in importance in elections and in government.
- In politics, they are both usually concealed behind the title of "political consultants."
- Both have been criticized in the media as being corruptive for the spirit of democracy (as one example, the 1997 movie *Wag the Dog*, directed by Barry Leviston and starring Robert de Niro and Dustin Hoffman).

Public relations is often reduced to media management (McNair, 1999); yet it needs to be understood as management of communication (Grunig and Hunt, 1984)–management of total communication (Theaker, 2001)–both internal (organizational, such as internal political party communication or campaign organization communication) and external (with journalists, but also broader with voters, supporters, contributors, etc.). As such it is a necessary complement to marketing.

Public relations stands for communication management and has four dimensions to consider (van Ruler et al., 2001; van Ruler and Verčič, 2002; Verčič et al., 2001):

A. *Managerial:* How to organize to communicate effectively and efficiently. Who, what, when and where is needed to connect with whom to produce a desired relationship to enable the targeted outcome? Good political communication is a complex managerial endeavor that involves many people and is an enterprise in itself.

B. Operational: How to use communication tools to their full potential. Prepare speeches, write press releases, stage press conferences, design Websites, make telephone calls, etc. These tasks are simple and often done by volunteers, but they need to be performed skillfully–only management complemented with proficient implementation brings success.

C. Educational: Candidates need to be educated and trained to perform on the stage, staff need to be educated and trained to perform in the backstage. Communication needs to be taught more than any other area of political life. Politicians acquire wisdom through life–they cannot be taught to become wise. For every technical issue, they have to rely on specialists. Yet, at the end of the day, it is them who must appear in front of journalists or the public at large.

D. Reflective: Not everything in politics is about winning elections, issues, and votes. It is also about values and norms. Candidates are not only responding to needs and demands of their target markets; moreover, to really make an impact, they also have to inspire and lead them. Reflective dimension of communication management refers to ability to shape one's political machinery into idealistic as much as into realistic and pragmatic tools to win votes. Without ideas politics collapses.

Political marketing and public relations can both be thought of as lubricants that enable political machinery to run smoothly. Without candidates and politicians being able to connect to their constituencies and learn on and about them, the political process becomes unidirectional, from top to the bottom. Without constituencies being able to educate themselves on their candidates and politicians, the political process becomes alienated and unable to impact.

In an effort to start a serious dialogue on the importance of understanding the interdependence of public relations and political marketing and the influence of both disciplines on politics, the 8th International Public Relations Research Symposium was devoted to this topic. The conference title was: "Politics of Communication and Communication of Politics: Cross-Cultural Theory Building in the Practice of Public Relations and Political Marketing" and was held in Vila Bled, Slovenia in July 2001. The aim was of the conference was twofold: First of all, to document the present relationships between politicians and communications professionals working in electoral committees, political parties, governments, government agencies, consultancies, polling agencies and other related organizations. Secondly, to examine antecedents and consequences of the increasing role of communication professionals in elections and government. The conference was organized by Pristop Communications in cooperation with PRSS, Public Relations Society of Slovenia and IABC Slovenia, and endorsed by CERP Education and Research and the European Association for Education & Research in Public Relations. The organizers of the conference were: Danny Moss (Manchester Metropolitan University), Dr. Dejan Verčič (Pristop Communications, Slovenia), Dr. Jon White (City University Business School, London) and Dr. Bruce I. Newman (DePaul University).

The conference attracted proposals from leading scholars and practitioners from several different countries. After an exhaustive review, 21 proposals were accepted on a competitive basis from professionals in nine different countries. The 21 papers presented at the conference covered a wide range of topics that addressed issues falling under the two dominant themes at the conference: Public relations and political marketing. Approximately 100 people participated in the conference from 18 different countries to gain insights into the intriguing marriage of these two disciplines. We sought to include those proposals that would help lead the participants of the two day conference towards some concrete conclusions that helped to lead to the development of this volume.

The first article by Philip John Davies (De Montford University, UK) discusses and illustrates the role of entrepreneurship, changing industrial technology, and the emergence of newly cost-effective materials as contexts for the creation of the wealth of campaign promotions that have adapted to change and maintained its place in the campaign for over 200 years.

The second article by David Deacon and Wendy Monk (Loughborough University, Leicestershire, UK) addresses the public communication activities of "Quangos" (Quasi-Autonomous Non-Governmental Organizations). Focusing mainly on news management strategies in the sector, they show that the popular image of quangos as highly introverted organizations needs revision, and that many place considerable emphasis on public communication issues. The next article by Jon White and Leslie de Chernatony (Birmingham University Business School, UK) examines the use made by political parties of branding as a means of establishing party values and winning political support. In the case of the British Labor Party they look in particular at the way in which political parties use communication to create, build and maintain political brands.

The article by Elaine Sherman (Hofstra University) and Leon Schiffman (St. John University) examines the dynamics of the expanding application and role of polls, focus groups and Internet-based research on political elections. They identify trends in terms of strategic and social outcomes. Selected examples in the article are drawn from the 2000 U.S. Presidential election as well as from the highly touted Clinton-Lazio New York Senatorial campaign.

The fifth article by Dennis W. Johnson (The George Washington University) looks at the 2000 U.S. Presidential election with a critical assessment of the strategies employed by the Bush and Gore organizations in the post-election period. The author concludes with some lessons that we can be learned from the closest contest in American history. In the article by Phil Harris (Manchester Metropolitan University, UK), a presentation is made of the results of an eight year research study in the UK and US that looks at the growth in party fundraising, ethics of the process, impact on the electoral system, candidates, parties, campaigning and methods of obtaining funds.

Kristina Plavšak (University of Ljubljana, Slovenia) explores the increasing inter-relation between governmental foreign affairs and diplomacy on one side, and media and public relations on the other side–how they started off in distinctly separate spheres and with different logic and how they seem to converge.

The last group of articles test a predictive model of voter behavior in three different countries: Slovenia, Poland and the United States. In the first test, Dejan Verčič and Iztok Verdnik (Pristop Communications, Slovenia) reported on a test of the model in Slovenia. They investigate the model in a different cultural and political setting from the one in which it was designed, and also in a different electoral setting–in a proportional instead of majority system of voting. The next test of the model by Andrzej Falkowski and Wojciech Cwalina (Warsaw School of Advanced Psychology and Catholic University of Lublin, Poland) analyze the data of the 2000 Polish elections. They reframe the model using a structural equation methodology and demonstrate how organizers of electoral campaigns can draw practical conclusions out of it. The last test of the model by Bruce I. Newman (DePaul University) studies the motivations behind a sample of voters who cast a ballot for George W. Bush and Al Gore in the 2000 U.S. Presidential campaign. The results reveal that each candidate successfully marketed himself to voters on the basis of very different values.

The ten contributions reported in this volume are original manuscripts based on the presentations made at the conference, and edited in an effort to bring together a mix of conceptual and empirical works from the fields of public relations and political marketing. It was our hope that the papers would address the issues of the conference theme from a cross-cultural perspective in an attempt to answer the following questions: Is contemporary politics anything more than public relations? How does the role of marketing change with respect to the development of a politician and his/her campaign platform in selected countries around the world? What kinds of political consultants are on the scene, and what are their roles, competencies and consequences of their work? Finally, is it possible to adapt the modeling of voter behavior from one country to another? We believe that the ideas advanced in this collection will serve to convince the readers that the fields of public relations and political marketing can work in an interdependent manner to advance the democratic form of government around the world.

CONFERENCE PARTICIPANTS

Ingri Assum (Norwegian Central Information Service, Norway)
Leislie de Chernatorny (University of Birmingham, United Kingdom)
Wojciech Cwalina (Catholic University of Lublin, Poland)
David Deacon (University of Loughborough, United Kingdom)
Philip John Davies (De Montfort University, United Kingdom)
Andrzej Falkowski (Catholic University of Lublin, Poland)
Anske F. Grobler (University of Pretoria, South Africa)
Phil Harris (Manchester Metropolitan University, United Kingdom)
Dennis W. Johnson (The George Washington University, U.S.A.)
Antonio Mira Marques Mendes (Polytechnic Institute of Lisbon, Portugal)
Wendy Monk (Loughborough University, United Kingdom)
Bruce I. Newman (DePaul University, U.S.A.)
Bozidar Novak (SPEM Communication Group, Slovenia)
Richard Phillipps (University of Western Sydney, Australia)
Kristina Plavšak (Faculty of Social Sciences, Slovenia)

Yannas Prodromos (Technological Educational Institution of Western Macedonia, Greece)
Juliet Roper (University of Waikato, New Zealand)
Judity-Rae Ross (DePaul University, U.S.A.)
Elaine Sherman (Hofstra University, U.S.A.)
Leon G. Schiffman (St. Johns University, U.S.A.)
Kevin Thomson (Marketing & Communication Agency Ltd., United Kingdom)
Mark A. Van Dyke (University of Maryland, U.S.A.)
Dominic Wring (University of Loughborough, United Kingdom)
Dejan Verčič (Pristop Communications, Slovenia)
Iztok Verdnik (Pristop Communications Slovenia)
Jon White (City University Business School, United Kingdom)

REFERENCES

Betteke van Ruler. *The Bled Manifesto on Public Relations.* Ljubljana: Pristop Communications, 2002.

Betteke van Ruler, Dejan Verčič, Bertil Flodin and Gerhard Buetschi. "Public relations in Europe: A kaleidoscopic picture." *Journal of Communication Management,* 6, No. 2, December 2001, p. 175.

Grunig, James E. and Todd Hunt. *Managing Public Relations.* New York: Holt, Rinehart & Winston, 1984.

McNair, Brian. *An Introduction to Political Communication,* 2. ed. London and New York: Routledge, 1999.

Newman, Bruce I. *The Marketing of the President: Political Marketing as Campaign Strategy.* Thousand Oaks, California: Sage Publications, 1994.

Newman, Bruce I. *Handbook of Political Marketing.* Sage Publications: Thousand Oaks, California, 1999a.

Newman, Bruce I. *The Mass Marketing of Politics: Democracy in an Age of Manufactured Images.* Sage Publications: Thousand Oaks, California,1999b.

Theaker, Alison. *Public Relations Handbook.* London and New York: Routledge, 2001.

Verčič, Dejan, Betteke van Ruler, Gerhard Bütschi and Bertil Flodin. "On the definition of public relations: A European view." *Public Relations Review,* 27, 2001, 373-387.

Bruce I. Newman, USA
Dejan Verčič, Slovenia

ARTICLES

The Material Culture of US Elections: Artisanship, Entrepreneurship, Ephemera and Two Centuries of Trans-Atlantic Exchange

Philip John Davies

De Montfort University

SUMMARY. The abiding motif of election campaigns in the USA is not the spot ad, nor the candidate debate, nor even the campaign Web site, but instead remains the campaign button. It should be consigned to his-

Philip John Davies, BA (Keele), MA (Essex), MA (Maryland), AcSS, is Professor of American Studies at De Montfort University and Director of the Eccles Centre for American Studies at the British Library, London, UK.

Address correspondence to: Philip John Davies, 20 Shirley Road, Leicester LE2 3LJ, England (E-mail: philip_davies@ntworld.com).

[Haworth co-indexing entry note]: "The Material Culture of US Elections: Artisanship, Entrepreneurship, Ephemera and Two Centuries of Trans-Atlantic Exchange." Davies, Philip John. Co-published simulta-neously in *Journal of Political Marketing* (The Haworth Political Press, an imprint of The Haworth Press, Inc.) Vol. 1, No. 2/3, 2002, pp. 9-24; and: *Communication of Politics: Cross-Cultural Theory Building in the Practice of Public Relations and Political Marketing* (eds: Bruce I. Newman, and Dejan Verčič) The Haworth Political Press, an imprint of The Haworth Press, Inc., 2002, pp. 9-24. Single or multiple copies of this article are available for a fee from The Haworth Document Delivery Service [1-800-HAWORTH, 9:00 a.m. - 5:00 p.m. (EST). E-mail address: getinfo@haworthpressinc.com].

10.1300/J199v01n02_02

9

tory by fast paced development of campaigns into modern technologies, but there are still hundreds of designs produced quadrennially for national campaigns, and many more for races at all levels. Even if the life of the campaign button is coming to a close, it has been a long run, from the brass buttons of 1789, to the tiny framed daguerreotypes of the mid-19th century, through the celluloid buttons of the 1890s, to the chip implanted versions of today.

But the campaign button is just the most ubiquitous example of the material culture of the US election. It has been modified by changes in artisan skills, industrial production, bulk availability, the changes in inexpensive materials and manufactures, and cost effectiveness and profitability. Over the same period of time many other artefacts have been used by entrepreneurs and campaigns to bring the candidates and their public together at the same time as making a profit–either financial or political. This article discusses the role of entrepreneurship, changing industrial technology, and the emergence of newly cost-effective materials, as contexts for the creation of the wealth of campaign ephemera that has adapted to change and maintained its place in the campaign for over 200 years. *[Article copies available for a fee from The Haworth Document Delivery Service: 1-800-HAWORTH. E-mail address: <getinfo@haworthpressinc. com> Website: <http://www.HaworthPress.com> © 2002 by The Haworth Press, Inc. All rights reserved.]*

KEYWORDS. US elections, history of elections, campaign materials, material culture

There was a dramatic fall in turnout at the 2001 UK general election. At 59.4% the voter turnout was down sharply from 71.5% in 1997, and 77.7% in 1992, the most recent previous elections, and the lowest turnout since 1918.[1] This fall in participation startled many observers, and some thought of it as another recent example of the Americanisation of British politics. Other topics within British politics that have attracted some attention as possible examples of Americanisation, or at least convergence towards some mid-Atlantic norm, have included the supposed increasingly presidential character of the prime minister's role; the growing influence of political consultants and personal advisers; the increasing similarity between the parties' free election broadcasts and US campaign ads; the weakening of ideology within political parties; and the weakening of ideological links between parties and the electorate.[2] While the trans-Atlantic element in these and other forms of "Americanisation" may at times be more imaginary than real, it is clear that political parties, candidates, and their advisers and strategists are very aware of international campaigns, and that their own efforts are informed by this context. As practitioners they look for effective tools and methods. As entrepreneurs they attempt to develop new products. And as message deliverers they attempt to build on the cultural foundations shared by their audience.

One apparent example of transatlantic influence was the modelling of a Conservative election broadcast on ads from the Republican anti-Dukakis campaign of 1988. The Conservative Party were allocated five television slots, each three-minutes long. Neither political parties nor candidates are allowed to purchase any television or radio time in addition to the official allocations. The Conservatives used two of these few slots to broadcast the same three-minute long party election broadcast alleging the Labour government's failure to tackle crime, and properly to enforce punishment. In particular the broadcast concentrated on the early release of criminals, and the numbers of these who re-offended, listing the violent crimes and rapes that had been detected among this group.

This Conservative Party broadcast appeared to be heavily influenced by two much briefer advertisements from the 1988 US campaign. The "Revolving Door" spot ad was created by the Bush/Quayle campaign. It used images of prisoners entering a corrections facility and then apparently leaving unimpeded through a gate similar to that used in a sports stadium. The ad attacked a prisoner furlough programme that had operated in Massachusetts during Democratic presidential candidate Michael Dukakis' gubernatorial term. Another spot ad in the 1988 campaign was financed by a Political Action Committee, supposedly independent of the official Bush/Quayle campaign, but making a supportive and parallel case against Dukakis. This political advertisement concentrated in particular on the prisoner furlough given to Willie Horton, who committed assault and rape while on leave from his Massachusetts prison. The Conservative 2001 broadcast seemed to draw heavily on these two spot ads: "[it] depicted men leaving prison under the early release scheme and immediately going on to commit fresh crimes. It included . . . a tally of crimes committed by prisoners released early, including two rapes."[3] The Conservative party political broadcast campaign seemed committed to this negative style, including one broadcast, ostensibly on education policy, picturing truant children burning vandalising cars and property, stealing, and drug-dealing. The

Conservative election team management seemed to have taken to heart the opinion of American campaigner Roger Ailes that "We are propagandists, not reporters,"[4] without acknowledging that such unremitting negativity might produce a back lash among commentators and voters.

Another trans-Atlantic reference may have been evident when a Conservative candidate, Oliver Letwin, claimed that the party would cut taxes by £20 billion. This figure implied deep public service cuts in the face of no evidence that the public were attracted by such slash and burn promises. The official Conservative policy was not so draconian, and the party leadership was very embarrassed by this slip. In the aftermath of his statement Letwin was suddenly unavailable for interview, as the Conservatives launched a damage-limitation exercise. The Labour Party response was to spend a day of the campaign asking "Where's Oliver Letwin?" complete with specially made posters, and targeted media events. This had echoes of Mitch McConnell's successful 1984 campaign to be US Senator from Kentucky, when his ads attacked the low profile of the incumbent, showing packs of bloodhounds running through Washington, and asking repeatedly "Where's Dee Huddleston?" The effort to maintain the embarrassment of Letwin and the Conservative Party was much less intense, but both the nature and speed of the Labour response had the mark of an adviser with awareness of American electoral history and practice. These influences could be unconscious. Many politicians and their advisers now have experience on both sides of the Atlantic. For example, Steve Morgan, liaison with foreign media for the Al Gore campaign, has also worked with the Labour Party, and in the aftermath of the Democrat's 2000 electoral failure he wrote of the trans-Atlantic lessons that could be learned.[5] In such a fluid political world campaign ideas can be transferred very easily.

If the UK has most recently been showing the influence of American campaign and cultural forms, campaign entrepreneurs do not only look west for inspiration. Larry Sabato points out that "The National Republican Congressional Committee was so impressed with the 1979 triumph of the GOP's political soulmate, the Conservative party, that it designed a $9.5 million television advertising effort airing in 1980 based on the humorous but hard-hitting Tory spots."[6] We may be able to intimate even earlier connections. Political philosopher Edmund Burke and New York City born Henry Cruger were elected Members of Parliament from Bristol, England, in 1774. A political favour now in the Museum of American Political Life at the University of Hartford, Connecticut, a kind of cockade of multicoloured silk, likely to have been red, white and blue before fading with age, is possibly from that election.[7] Few political favours of this kind have survived, though newspapers of the late eighteenth century often mention such items. The Victoria and Albert Museum in London has handkerchiefs from earlier dates printed with political subjects, and a ribbon produced for a royal wedding in 1733. Metal tokens celebrating political events and celebrities were also popular in England. So there is a documented tradition of artisan produced celebratory materials relating to political opinion and regime support. Homemade and manufactured items used local skills to combine contemporary materials and media to good effect, producing items that proclaimed support, and presumably, in the case of mass produced items such as handkerchiefs, turned a profit for some local entrepreneur.

One can recognise the resemblance between the Burke/Cruger cockade, and the modern British political rosette, much in evidence on British election nights, but perhaps it and its fellow British political favours of the eighteenth century also provide a route to the American campaign button. Cruger, variously the Member of Parliament for Bristol and Mayor of Bristol between 1774 and 1790, later returned to his birthplace and was elected to the New York State Senate in 1792. Many other early American leaders and citizens of the young nation had trans-Atlantic experience and perhaps this had some influence on the development of political favours in the USA.

The Presidential election of 1789 was something of a nationalist celebration. It spawned a number of souvenirs as the button makers of New York and Connecticut commemorated the first presidency. These first American political tokens were produced by entrepreneurs for commercial reasons, exploiting the technology of the day. Few manufactured items were cheap in the eighteenth century, but buttons were a medium that could take and display a message, and they were relatively accessible to the interested population. These were genuine, utilisable buttons–not the pinback badges that carry the same name. Various designs were impressed on brass buttons–the new president's initials, a chain linking the states' initials, and an eagle and sunrise design that Washington is reputed to have worn at his inauguration–and similar inscriptions appeared on hatbands and on sashes.

Framed glass brooches containing a cameo or an engraved picture of the President were also popular in the late 18th and early 19th centuries and the market was good enough that some political issue items were imported. The English manufacturer of fine china, Wedgwood, perhaps created the most lasting image. A chained slave printed on a plate in the 1790s featured the telling slogan "Am I not a Man and a Brother"–by the early nineteenth century the image had been re-used in many forms and media, and had segued into a female form, "Am I not a Woman and a Sister" appealing both to abolitionist and suffragist sensitivities.[8]

The first US presidential election when medals advertising support for a candidate were worn by supporters may have been that of 1824. Some scholars are leery of the claim that these were the first "official campaign buttons." Contemporary newspaper reports and advertisements suggest that any such medallion production was likely to have been small-scale and still of the souvenir trade variety. Andrew Jackson had gained the most popular votes and Electoral College votes in 1824, but failed to gain an absolute majority in the Electoral College. The House of Representatives, behaving entirely properly within the constitutional rules, but perhaps with an insensitivity to the increasingly powerful opinion of the general electorate, selected John Quincy Adams, to serve as president. The bitter rematch election of 1828 stimulated the production of a variety of medals and other trinkets aimed directly at the camps of the major candidates, and the political debate of the period included a vitriolic negativism.[9]

Jackson's vigorous pursuit of the White House, the strong opposition he provoked, and the considerable extension of the franchise in presidential elections, changed the campaign. One review of surviving 1828 materials claims that "Jackson's matrimonial affairs, his profanity, his gamecocks and race horses, his duels and brawls, were the subject of merciless campaign propaganda. Handbills with pictures of coffins of soldiers executed by Jackson were distributed by Clay."[10] Jackson's supporters replied in kind with accusations that Quincy Adams had installed "gambling furniture" in the White House–a billiard table.

Into the mid-nineteenth century electioneering materials rapidly developed in varied forms–using the available technologies and artisan skills of the nation to spread the campaign. Candidates' names, pictures and messages appeared on paper, textiles, metal, ceramics, glass, and any material that could be pressed into action, and justify cost of production. The lithographed "silk" was common: ribbons printed with pictures or messages for or against positions and candidates were used as bookmarks, or be pinned to a lapel.[11]

Newspapers played an important part from the earliest American elections, but in 1840 a newspaper item impacted on the campaign and on campaign ephemera. *The Baltimore Republican* lampooned Whig candidate William Henry Harrison, saying, "Give him a barrel of hard cider and a pension of two thousand a year, and . . . he will sit the remainder of his days in a log cabin."[12] This contempt for simple pleasures and hard life was an enormous miscalculation in a nation where both the franchise and the frontier were expanding rapidly. It gave the Whigs slogans, symbols and campaign image that would transfer into many available media. Campaign spin meisters swiftly fabricated a log cabin origin for Harrison. He did own one. It is possible his parents lived in one temporarily while their charming and comfortable house was being built. It was not his birthplace, nor had it ever been his residence, but it transferred very well into many media, and was a symbol of humility and democracy that lodged comfortably in the public mind.

The log cabin turned up as a ceramic item, on the reverse of Harrison medallion, it looked pretty good overprinted on a flag, and stood out clearly when etched on to a traditional silk. Log cabins were built on street corners, wheeled around towns, and formed the centre of political celebrations (presumably cider played its part too), and the log cabin to White House legend was established, to make repeated appearances in presidential elections thereafter. This outburst of campaign activity so put out the Democratic Party that its 1844 platform contained a plank condemning "factitious symbols," and "displays and appeals insulting to the judgement, and subversive of the intellect of the people."[13] This had no practical effect as campaigners and entrepreneurs continued to produce a wide variety of novelties.

In the mid-nineteenth century, political entrepreneurs and reporters alike had plenty of candidates and controversy to fire an interest in their goods. It was a time of multi-party activity, when even a former president, Millard Fillmore, contributed to the fluctuating variations in political movements, in 1856 becoming the candidate of the strangely identified Know-Nothings. The ubiquitous campaign medallions seemed to lend candidate profiles a rather heroic representation, although as John C. Fremont found in 1856, a silhouette that looked especially good in this kind of representation was no guarantee of victory. Fremont was also one of those presidential hopefuls were already well aware of the value of wrapping themselves in the flag–using the US flag as a background for a display of candidate names. The political items seen in the run up to the American Civil War demonstrated little sign of potential reconciliation, and illustrated the sharp and bitter divisions between regions, parties, and their nominees.

In 1860 the political parties split as never before. Eager to get into a burgeoning market the manufacturers could sometimes make mistakes– one silk appeared with the eventual winner's name mis-spelled "Abram" Lincoln, but silks were slipping out of fashion, and campaign medals and badges were becoming increasingly popular. *Harper's Magazine* recalled the campaign of 1860:

> . . . the manufacturers all made money because of so many candidates in the field and because of the intense interest. Nearly everybody wore a medal then and there was no difficulty in telling how a man stood. The nearest approach to a button in the . . . campaign was the first appearance of a medal-like affair which held in place tin-type photographs of the candidates. Lincoln and his running mate Hannibal Hamlin were pictured on opposite sides of the republican medal. The same manufacturers also turned out these things for other parties.[14]

At the same time torch-lit street parades in an increasingly urban nation expanded opportunities for campaign ephemera. Supporters carried banners and torches–metal canisters, often in symbolic shapes, containing fuel, with a lighted wick, attached to a stick. Candidate parades were often identified by marchers wearing similar slick oilcloth capes–which might have been as much to protect them from the kerosene dripping from torches.

During the last quarter of the nineteenth century campaigns reflected the economic and demographic shift to cities and factories. Campaign items became functional, and representative of the prevalent style and taste, and of changing methods of production. Mass production brought oil lamps, cast iron matchholders, Japanese lanterns, umbrellas, cut-throat razors, glassware, canes, toys, iron door stops, china and household items into the election market. Bandannas were popular, although they were generally designed to display rather than to wear.

Such items were used to lampoon politicians too. The excesses of New York's authoritarian and self-serving Tammany Hall group of politicians prompted a metal money box which featured a Tammany politician in a throne-like chair. When a coin was placed in his outstretched hand, he bowed graciously and slipped it into his pocket. With a certain equity of antagonism, it was around this time that Thomas Nast's acid newspaper cartoons attached the donkey and the elephant irrevocably to the two major parties. Eventually the parties accepted the satires as a useful label, and ran with their assigned animals.

If the second half of the nineteenth century was primarily a time when existing campaign technology was adapted and elaborated, the end of the century brought a dramatic shift of gear. Campaigning for President was becoming expensive. Under the direction of Mark Hanna the 1896 McKinley general election campaign spent \$3,350,000 (not including prenomination costs). Hanna worked for a 1896 McKinley victory over many years. He had shepherded McKinley on speaking tours, opened a "McKinley for President" office on the fringes of the 1892 Republican convention, opened a permanent national HQ in Chicago in spring 1895. He arranged a speakers bureau of 1,400 GOP supporters, and the campaign is reputed to have distributed over 200 million pieces of literature in English, German, French, Spanish, Italian, Norwegian, Swedish, Danish, French and Hebrew. Not until 1920 did a Republican presidential candidate again spend as much, and no Democrat reached this total before 1928. Indeed, it is only since 1952 that both candidates have consistently, simultaneously, and, as it turns out, exponentially, spent more than the 1896 McKinley total.[15]

The main technological breakthrough was the invention of the celluloid covered campaign button. Whitehead and Hoag, in 1894, began using thin, clear, celluloid as a covering for paper designs. They were heat-bonded and mounted onto a metal disc, with a pin back fitted inside the curl of the button.[16] There was no better time for this invention–campaign enthusiasm was high, and mass-made buttons cheap. Both 1896 candidates, McKinley and Bryan, inspired hundreds of designs. According to a contemporary observer, "campaign buttons adorn the lapels of voters all over the land."[17]

The turn of the century campaigns in the USA may have produced the greatest variety of genuine campaign items of any time, as nineteenth century artisan variety met twentieth century mass production. Milk jugs had candidate faces painted on them, deodorant bottles wore labels similarly decorated, mechanical badges in the form of gold or silver bugs displayed the candidates' features on opened wings when their carapaces were pressed, a pair of gilt skeleton shaped lapel pins carried the candidates' pictures in their rib-cages, and silks were produced for special occasions, for example, to commemorate the delegations who visited the McKinley front porch on trips subsidised by Republican-supporting railway companies.

William Jennings Bryan, a noted orator, broke with the traditional reserve of presidential candidacy, and took his campaigns to the people, stumping the country from the rear of a railway train. Charismatic and energetic candidates made sure that the move to active campaigning took hold quickly and permanently. If ever there had been a mould of diffident campaigning, it was now broken, even though later candidates have been known to try to stick to their porches, or, as the case may be, their Rose Gardens.

If ever there had been an earlier mould of diffident campaigning, it was now broken. Radio came into the living room. In 1924, $120,000 was spent by the Republicans, and $40,000 by the Democrats on radio ads, four years later both parties combined spent over $1 million.[18] Traditional items were not eclipsed, and the lapel button was still the main token for politics of all stripes. They were cheap to produce and give away–even cheaper after the introduction of lithograph pinbacks in 1920–and virtually any contribution they elicited was profit.

The year 1940 provoked probably the biggest battle of campaign buttons as Wendell Willkie stormed through 34 states in 51 days, attacking almost everything about Roosevelt. Sloganeering buttons carried the anti-Roosevelt campaign to the lapels of Republicans across the nations. A button saying "Dr. Jekyll from Hyde Park," mixing the reference from popular literature (and horror film) with the name of the Roosevelt family home, was pretty direct. "We Don't Want Eleanor Either" put the "first family" on a button, and confirmed its place at centre stage. The decision by Franklin Roosevelt to break with tradition and become the first candidate to challenge for a third consecutive term in the White House attracted most attention. One button carried the slogan "No Crown for Franklin," attacking the supposed near monarchical designs of Roosevelt. Another button bluntly pointed out that "No Man is Indispensable," and with a frankness that might have been surprising over sixty years ago, the 1940 button saying "No Man Can Be Good Three Times" came close to the bone.

Also in 1940 television coverage of the political conventions was broadcast to an audience of 100,000 viewers. In 1948 Truman and Dewey purchased TV time to broadcast speeches. In 1950, after viewing the first known filmed campaign ad, for a Maryland Democrat, President Truman advised him to save his money and go and shake 10,000 hands instead. Only two years later television had reached one-third of American households, and the first presidential spot ads were shown, the two parties spending $3.5 million on electronic media in that campaign, and the Republicans massively outspending the Democrats.

With the growing role of the electronic media, however, major election artists emerged, especially in television. The start was simple, homely and jaunty. The spots reflected the jingles common in early television advertising. But it was not long before substantial dramatic steps were taken. The most famous US election advertisement of all time was probably that commissioned by the Doyle, Dane, Bernbach agency for the Johnson campaign in 1964, and made by Tony Schwartz, "The daisy girl." The little girl plucks the petals from a daisy, counting inaccurately. The frame freezes, an echo-enhanced male voice starts a countdown. The camera zooms in on the girl's iris. As the camera reaches the black depths of the little girl's eye, the countdown reaches zero, and an atomic mushroom cloud erupts. Johnson, in a text borrowed in part from W. H. Auden, intones "We must live together, or we must die . . . The stakes are too high for you to stay home." The advertisement was shown only once or twice before Goldwater protests resulted in it being withdrawn. But it was discussed repeatedly on the news broadcasts and in the print media. It fed well on public concern that one of the candidates might make a trigger-happy President if elected.

For large election campaigns TV is essential, and the competition is not just the opposing candidate, but all other TV advertising. Now advocacy and independent ads are made by many groups, as campaigns attract an increasing variety of political entrepreneurs, but even though cable and satellite TV have introduced narrowcasting, with targeted ads for differentiated audiences electronic mass media campaigns seem qualitatively different to those methods of contact that leave you with a button, bumper sticker, silly hat, tee shirt, soap, pen, or even chewing gum, jelly sweets, or a small bag of carrots.[19]

The Internet began to produce a new category of political ephemera in the 1990s. Campaigns increasingly use the Web as part of their campaign. The appeal is similar to previous communications tools of American democracy–the Internet is the latest cost-effective campaign tool. It is cheaper to use than the phone, mail, print or any other tangible medium. It can deliver text, pictures, photos, posters (to be printed at the recipients' cost), sound and video. It is a medium that lends itself to the small-scale political entrepreneur as well as the major operation–the home-made and the artisan can perform alongside the big budget production.[20]

Certainly all major candidate campaigns were using the Internet by 2000, but it is not only they who are affected by a format that one journalist US typified as political steroids–allowing candidates to run faster with less effort and more power. It is twenty years since Vietnam draft resister David McReynolds first ran for president, but it is unlikely that he has every previously been able to manage the exposure that the Socialist Party of the USA Website could engender in the 2000 election. Nonetheless one cannot yet wear a personal computer on a lapel, so candidate sites offer for sale the traditional favours of the campaign. The Libertarian Party's 2000 candidate for president, Harry Browne, squared the circle by selling from his Website a button which includes the address of his Website.

The UK election of 2001 showed similar technological shifts in campaigning to those found in recent US elections, although its reliance on the non-technological handcounting of votes on this occasion delivered a definitive result more quickly than its American counterpart. The New Labour campaign effort in 2001 also launched one advertising initiative that was very self-consciously aware of the context and conventions of the contemporary trans-Atlantic culture of movies. A series of three billboard posters used cinematic images to attack the Conservative Party and its leadership. "Towering Inflation Rates" parodied *Towering Inferno*, by no means a contemporary movie, but a TV repeat favourite. The viewing public is very conversant with the visual conventions of the disaster movie poster, which were here used to warn of disastrous policies if the opposition were to take office. Even the use of slightly dated filmic images might have been calculated to remind the viewing public of those earlier times (actually not as long ago as the film genres being used) when the Conservatives were a government so bad that the electorate threw them out with a resounding vote of no confidence.

The Labour poster "Economic Disaster II" used the convention of the movie sequel, well-known to the film-literate voter, all of whom know that follow ups are usually worse than the original. Conservative leaders Michael Portillo and William Hague starred on the billboard as "Mr. Boom" and "Mr. Bust," a strap line threatened that these Tories might be "Coming to a home, hospital, school and business near you," and, in case the viewer was thinking it was safe to go back into the water, the poster warned "Don't go back." "Return of the Repossessed" capitalised on the vogue for the Horror genre, while recalling alleged problems of the former Conservative administration. Horror may be in vogue, but is still either frightening or funny (or both), and New Labour's playing of this card was doubly rewarded when Baroness Thatcher, on the campaign trail, referred to the poster, showed her own connectedness with what was playing in British cinemas, and reminded voters precisely of the fears on which the campaign was attempting to build, that "The Mummy has Returned." This phase of the campaign was not subtle, and a Labour party election broadcast spent another three minutes hammering home the cinematically veneered message of these posters, but this effort combined billboards, posters, and electronic and Internet media above all to show the entrepreneurial adaptation of new and old technologies and trans-Atlantic cultural influences to impact on the local cultural context of the contemporary election.

The shift to major election campaigns being dominated by electronic media and communications will not be reversed, but even in technology-driven America it has not sounded the death knell of traditional campaign events and items. The primary season, especially in Iowa and New Hampshire, as well as the vagaries of the Electoral College system, newly impressed by the tightly fought election of 2000, require some traditional campaigning from presidential candidates. Nostalgia can always play a part in a campaign, and traditional campaign items are appreciated especially by those loyalists who make up the essential and hard-working volunteer staff of campaigns.[21] And with about half a million elected offices to fill there is always likely to be a place for traditional materials, using the low-cost technologies: handmade signs, printed signs, car decorations, stickers, bubblegum cigars, toy noisemakers, jewellery, watches, cosmetic aids, emery boards, dolls, puppets, mugs, glasses, and other domestic items have all been used in recent elections.

Politicians, for the sake of their careers, and in the forceful pursuit of their ideas, will continue to adapt their styles to the changing political, cultural and technological environment in which they campaign. They are competing in the market for public attention against rival politicians, and against all the other commercial, entertainment, and news messages being projected, and market share is not enough. Entrepreneurs will continue to take advantage of the sales they can make on top of a vital campaign. And they will all continue to exploit new materials, design and technologies to inject the maximum excitement into the campaign. But the paraphernalia of street-level politicking continues to be powerful and accessible, and for some time to come it may not to be the spot ad, the candidate debate, nor even the candidate Web site, but the campaign button that remains the motif of the overwhelming excitement of US election campaigns.

NOTES

1. For coverage of the 2001 UK election, see, for example, David Butler and Dennis Kavanagh, eds., *The British General Election of 2001* (Basingstoke: Palgrave, 2002); Pippa Norris, ed., *Britain Votes 2001* (Oxford: Oxford University Press, 2001).

2. See, for example, Michael Foley, *The Rise of the British Presidency* (Manchester: Manchester University Press, 1993); Dennis Kavanagh, *Election Campaigning: The New Marketing of Politics* (Oxford: Blackwell, 1995); Bob Franklin, *Packaging Politics: Political Communications in Britain's Media Democracy* (London: Edward Arnold, 1994).

3. Butler and Kavanagh, p. 151.

4. Quoted in Frank I. Luntz, *Candidates, Consultants and Campaigns* (New York: Basil Blackwell, 1988), p. 105.

5. Steve Morgan, "Exclusive: How Labour Could Lose," *New Statesman*, 12 February 2001, pp. 8-10.

5. Larry Sabato, *The Rise of Political Consultants: New Ways of Winning Elections* (New York: Basic Books, 1981), p. 62.

7. The author was introduced to this item by Dr. Edmund B. Sullivan, Founder Director of the Museum of American Political Life, University of Hartford, and author of many publications on American political items, including *Collecting Political Americana* (Hanover, MA: Christopher Publishing, 1991).

8. *Wedgwood Portraits and the American Revolution* (London and Washington D.C.: National Portrait Gallery and Smithsonian Institution, 1976), pp. 116-7.

9. On these early campaigns see, for example, Michael J. Heale, *The Presidential Quest: Candidates and Images in American Political Culture, 1786-1852* (London: Longman, 1982); Richard P. McCormick, *The Presidential Game* (New York: Oxford University Press, 1982); and Gil Troy, *See How They Ran: The Changing Role of the Presidential Candidate* (New York: The Free Press, 1991).

10. Edmund B. Sullivan, *America Goes to the Polls* (Hartford, CT: Travelers Insurance Company, 1964), p. 1.

11. Illustrations of many kinds of US political ephemera can be found, for example, in: Roger A. Fischer, *Tippecanoe and Trinkets Too: The Material Culture of American Political Campaigns, 1828-1984* (Urbana, IL: University of Illinois Press, 1988); Beryl Frank, *The Pictorial History of the Democratic Party* (Secaucus, NJ: Castle Books, 1980); Beryl Frank, *The Pictorial History of the Republican Party* (Secaucus, NJ: Castle Books, 1980); Edmund B. Sullivan, *Hell-Bent for the White House* (Hartford. CT: Museum of American Political Life, 1988).

12. Lillian B. Miller et al., *'If Elected . . .': Unsuccessful Candidates for the Presidency, 1796-1968* (Washington D.C.: Smithsonian Institution Press, 1972), p. 124.

13. Heale, p. 107.

14. " 'Campaign medals: Relics of political contests that were waged before the (civil) war,' an article reprinted from *Harper's Magazine*-1896," reprinted in *Keynoter*, 86, no. 2 (1986): 34-5.

15. Stephen Wayne, *The Road to the White House 1996: The Politics of Presidential Elections* (New York: St. Martin's Press, 1996), 29, 32; Roger Fischer, "Prosperity's Advance Agent: Wm. McKinley and the gold standard," *Keynoter*, 84, no. 2 (1984): 9.

16. Fischer, *Tippecanoe*, pp. 144-5.

17. George Dollar, "Campaign buttons," originally published in the *Strand* (1896), republished in *Keynoter*, 84, no. 2 (1984): 20-2.

18. Robert J. Dinkin, *Campaigning in America: A History of Election Practices* (New York: Greenwood Press, 1989), p. 132.

19. Many of the items described here and throughout this article are from the author's archive of election materials. This archive is in the process of transfer to the Rothermere American Institute at the University of Oxford, ultimately to be made accessible to scholars for research purposes. The carrots were distributed on primary election day 1998 by a candidate for local office in Boston who was using the slogan 'Keene–the candidate with vision.'

20. To explore the Internet manifestations of the 2000 US election see: *http://archive0.alexa.com/collections/e2k.html* an archive of 800 gigabytes of information.

21. Louis Sandy Maisel, *From Obscurity to Oblivion: Running in the Congressional Primary* (Knoxville, TN: University of Tennessee Press, 1982), p. 113.

BIBLIOGRAPHY

Butler, David and Dennis Kavanagh, eds., *The British General Election of 2001.* Basingstoke: Palgrave, 2002.

" 'Campaign medals: Relics of political contests that were waged before the (civil) war,' an article reprinted from *Harper's Magazine*–1896," reprinted in *Keynoter*, 86, no. 2 (1986): 34-5.

Dinkin, Robert J., *Campaigning in America: A History of Election Practices.* New York: Greenwood Press, 1989.

Dollar, George, "Campaign buttons," originally published in the *Strand* (1896), republished in *Keynoter*, 84, no. 2 (1984): 20-2.

Fischer, Roger, "Prosperity's Advance Agent: Wm. McKinley and the Gold Standard," *Keynoter*, 84, no. 2 (1984): 9-11.

Fischer, Roger A., *Tippecanoe and Trinkets too: The Material Culture of American Political Campaigns, 1828-1984.* Urbana, IL: University of Illinois Press, 1988.

Foley, Michael, *The Rise of the British Presidency.* Manchester: Manchester University Press, 1993.

Frank, Beryl, *The Pictorial History of the Democratic Party.* Secaucus, NJ: Castle Books, 1980.

Frank, Beryl, *The Pictorial History of the Republican Party.* Secaucus, NJ: Castle Books, 1980.

Franklin, Bob, *Packaging Politics: Political Communications in Britain's Media Democracy.* London: Edward Arnold, 1994.

Heale, Michael J., *The Presidential Quest: Candidates and Images in American Political Culture, 1786-1852.* London: Longman, 1982.

Kavanagh, Dennis, *Election Campaigning: The New Marketing of Politics.* Oxford: Blackwell, 1995.

Luntz, Frank I., *Candidates, Consultants and Campaigns.* New York: Basil Blackwell, 1988.

Maisel, Louis Sandy, *From Obscurity to Oblivion: Running in the Congressional Primary.* Knoxville, TN: University of Tennessee Press, 1982.

McCormick, Richard P., *The Presidential Game.* New York: Oxford University Press, 1982.

Miller, Lillian B., Beverly J. Cox, Frederick S. Voss, Jeanette M. Hussey, and Judith S. King, *'If Elected . . .': Unsuccessful Candidates for the Presidency, 1796-1968.* Washington D.C.: Smithsonian Institution Press, 1972.

Morgan, Steve, "Exclusive: How Labour Could Lose." *New Statesman*, 12 February 2001, pp. 8-10.

Norris, Pippa, ed., *Britain Votes 2001.* Oxford: Oxford University Press, 2001.

Sabato, Larry, *The Rise of Political Consultants: New Ways of Winning Elections*. New York: Basic Books, 1981.

Sullivan, Edmund B., *America Goes to the Polls* (Hartford, CT: Travelers Insurance Company, 1964).

Sullivan, Edmund B., *Hell-Bent for the White House* (Hartford, CT: Museum of American Political Life, 1988).

Sullivan, Edmund B., *Collecting Political Americana*. Hanover, MA: Christopher Publishing, 1991.

Troy, Gil, *See How They Ran: The Changing Role of the Presidential Candidate*. New York: The Free Press, 1991.

Wayne, Stephen, *The Road to the White House 1996: The Politics of Presidential Elections*. New York: St. Martin's Press, 1996.

Wedgwood Portraits and the American Revolution. London and Washington D.C.: National Portrait Gallery and Smithsonian Institution, 1976.

News Management
and New Managerialism:
Quangos and Their Media Relations

David Deacon
Wendy Monk

Loughborough University, England

SUMMARY. This article examines the public communication activities of "Quangos" (Quasi-Autonomous Non-Governmental Organizations). These non-elected organizations fulfill diverse public functions–such as, providing services, advising policy makers, regulating other institutions, representing the interests of certain social and cultural groups, supporting private enterprise, and promoting pro-social values and practices.

Focusing mainly on news management strategies in the sector, the article shows that the popular image of quangos as highly introverted organizations needs revision, and that many place considerable emphasis on public communication issues. However, this recognition contextualises rather than invalidates concerns about accountability within this tier of government, as publicity activities in the sector are geared towards facilitating the external promotion of organizations' roles rather than scrutiny of their conduct. *[Article copies available for a fee from The Haworth Document Delivery Service:*

David Deacon is Senior Lecturer in Communication and Media Studies and Wendy Monk is Former Research Associate at the Communication Research Centre, Department of Social Sciences, Loughborough University, Leicestershire, England, LE11 3TU (E-mail: d.n.deacon@lboro.ac.uk).

[Haworth co-indexing entry note]: "News Management and New Managerialism: Quangos and Their Media Relations." Deacon, David, and Wendy Monk. Co-published simultaneously in *Journal of Political Marketing* (The Haworth Political Press, an imprint of The Haworth Press, Inc.) Vol. 1, No. 2/3, 2002, pp. 25-44; and: *Communication of Politics: Cross-Cultural Theory Building in the Practice of Public Relations and Political Marketing* (eds: Bruce I. Newman, and Dejan Verčič) The Haworth Political Press, an imprint of The Haworth Press, Inc., 2002, pp. 25-44. Single or multiple copies of this article are available for a fee from The Haworth Document Delivery Service [1-800-HAWORTH, 9:00 a.m. - 5:00 p.m. (EST). E-mail address: getinfo@haworthpressinc.com].

10.1300/J199v01n02_03

KEYWORDS. Government, Quangos, media relations, news management, publicity, United Kingdom

INTRODUCTION

This article examines the news management and public relations activities of "quangos" in Britain (Quasi-Autonomous Non-Governmental Organisations).[1] The term was conceived as a joke in the 1960s, but has since gained international currency as a label for public bodies that are created by government to operate semi-independently under the guidance of political appointees. These non-elected organisations fulfil diverse public functions–for example, providing services, advising policy makers, regulating other institutions, representing the interests of certain social and cultural groups, supporting private enterprise, and promoting pro-social values and practices.

A central purpose of this article is to develop links between two debates that have attracted considerable debate but which to date have not been effectively connected. The first concerns the spread of "promotionalism" (Wernick, 1991) and the increasingly significant role of the media in the conduct of political business in nations such as Britain (Mazzolena and Schultz, 1999). These processes are most evident in the electoral arena, but are just the tip of the iceberg. As a consequence of broader political, social and fiscal uncertainties, diverse private and public institutions are becoming ever more concerned with image maintenance and achieving a prominent and positive media presence.

The second issue concerns the changing structure of governing institutions in countries like Britain, and in particular the exponential expansion of "appointive government" over recent decades (Skelcher, 1998). According to one estimate, quangos now control a collective budget of £60.4 billion in the UK: representing a third of all public expenditure and a 45 percent real term increase since 1979 (Weir and Hall, 1996). Another estimate projects that local appointees now outnumber locally elected politicians (Davis, 1996: 2). These changes have prompted debate about their broader democratic and constitutional implications. To whom are these public bodies accountable? Is their "arms-length" relationship with government illusory–a smoke screen for enacting government policy beyond parliamentary and public redress? Do they represent a more efficient and independent means for organising public business? Who gets appointed to positions of authority in these public bodies, and on what basis? Are these organisations at the root of a growing "democratic deficit" in our political system?

The media have a crucial role to play in both relaying and stimulating this vital discourse (Negrine, 1996: 11, Gay, 1996: 43). But to date there has been no systematic investigation of the media relations in this expanding tier of government. Although some have speculated about the possible barriers that hinder effective media appraisal, we know very little about how developed exchange relationships are between these public bodies and the mainstream media. This reveals a general blind spot within mainstream political communication research, where attention has remained so fixated on the *conduct* of electoral processes, that scant consideration has been given to the implications of structural changes in government that have significantly eroded the *jurisdiction* of the electorate (Deacon and Monk, 2000).

COMPLEMENTARITY OR CONTRADICTION? SECRECY AND PUBLICITY IN QUASI-GOVERNMENT

The mid-1990s witnessed a brief but intense public debate about the role of quasi government in Britain. The roots of this "great quango panic" (Whitehead, 1995) lay in wider concerns about governmental sleaze, the material proliferation of quangos through the 1980s, and the timely interventions of an informal coalition of academics, politicians and pressure groups (Deacon and Monk, 2000). A central theme in this debate was that endemic secrecy among quangos prevented any effective monitoring of quangos' activities, not least by journalists (Marr, 1995: 96). Many of these assertions were based on two connections that were taken as axiomatic. Because quangos' political authority is bestowed by the government rather than the electorate, they were assumed to lack any incentive to care whether public or other non-state sources knew of their activities or held them in esteem. Furthermore, as there were few official requirements for quangos to be open about their activities, it was taken that these opportunities for inscrutability and secrecy were widely exploited.

In the wake of the political furore, a succession of official measures followed to open up quangos' activities to public appraisal. For example, in 1998 the new Labour government published a series of recommendations derived from a public consultation process initiated by the 1997 Green Paper "Opening Up Quangos." These included that all officially recognised quangos should consult with the public more directly, produce annual reports and communicate their roles more effectively.

In this article the popular conception of quangos as closed and secretive organisations is scrutinised rather than accepted on face value, as there are grounds for suspecting that the actual situation is more complex than has been suggested. Although quangos are not publicly elected, many fulfil highly significant public roles–delivering key services, regulating institutions, promoting good practice, facilitating institutional and public partnerships, and so on. Given this sort of engagement it seems implausible that all quangos can be as oblivious of their wider political context as some claim. Furthermore, very few, if any, organisations operate in a state of complete secrecy. As Downing comments, "Secrecy is not used as an impermeable shield blotting out all communication, but as a device to allow the pinnacle of the power structure to communicate how and when it prefers" (1986: 14). Recognition of this point shifts the focus away from a model of total disengagement towards one that is more attuned to analysing the terms of external engagement. Opening up these questions does not deny the validity of concerns about secrecy and freedom of information, it contextualises them–revealing them as part of the picture, rather than the entirety.

Before presenting the research findings it is necessary to explain how "quangos" were defined for the purposes of the analysis.

DEFINING QUASI-GOVERNMENT

Defining "quangos" in a British context is a matter of dispute. The confusion is partly due to the imprecision of the term, partly because of the improvised nature of the British government which has long confounded stable categorisation, and crucially because "quango counting" is such a contentious political matter. For example, a highly restricted definition of quasi-government (i.e., only officially "recognised" public bodies, such as Executive and Advisory Non-Departmental Bodies, Boards of Visitors and Tribunals) suggests a steady annual reduction in appointive bodies in Britain since the early 1980s (Cabinet Office, 1999).

Our research adopted an extensive definition of quasi-government, covering "recognised" and "non recognised" agencies. Most non-recognised quangos are "local public spending bodies" and NHS bodies, but we also included organisations that are mentioned in official lists of "Public Bodies" and display some of the classic qualities of appointive government (e.g., an "arms length" relationship with central government and statutory powers with no direct electoral mandate). These additional agencies are: "Next Step" agencies, official regulators, Nationalised Industries and Public Corporations. Overseas or supra-national agencies that might be categorised as "quangos" were excluded.

A broad definition of appointive government was adopted for several reasons. We wanted to compare media relations between "recognised" and "non-recognised" sectors. As non-recognised agencies are at the root of the expansion of appointive government, it would have been remiss to ignore publicity activities in these emergent governmental forms. A preliminary analysis of selected media reports revealed that journalists apply the term "quango" widely and unpredictably across all of the organisational types covered by this research. Finally, we are more convinced by the theoretical arguments for an extensive definition of quangos.

RESEARCH DETAILS

This analysis of quangos' publicity and media activities is based on two related empirical exercises. The first was a questionnaire-based random sample survey of 274 UK quangos, conducted between May and July 1999. The survey achieved a 70.5 percent response rate from an initial random selection of 390 agencies. The second source of evidence is 61 interviews conducted with senior personnel responsible for the communication and publicity activities of a diverse range of these public bodies. Interviewee selection reflected (a) the diversity of quangos covered by the research, and (b) differing levels of media exposure (high/low).

THE EXTENT OF QUANGOS' NEWS MANAGEMENT AND PUBLICITY ACTIVITIES

Sixty-eight percent of organisations that responded to the survey had at least one member of staff with formally designated responsibilities for media and/or publicity activities. Thirty-two percent of organisations had "information officers" and 33 percent had staff involved in "publications" either in addition to, or instead of, media and publicity staff. Overall, 74 percent of agencies had staff with responsibilities in at least one of these capacities. The agencies least likely to have these staff were Advisory NDPBs (13 percent), Tribunals and Boards of Visitors (36 percent) and Housing Associations (47 percent).

In structural terms, most quangos did not demarcate media relations from other PR and marketing activities and emphasised multi-skilling. However, there was little evidence such conflation was due to widespread under-resourcing for media and publicity work. Fifty-six percent of respondents felt funding in this areas was "fairly adequate," compared with 29 percent who said it was "fairly inadequate," 9 percent who said it was "completely adequate," and 4 percent that said "completely inadequate" (1 percent weren't able to judge). This picture of modest satisfaction was echoed in most opinions expressed in the interviews.

Table 1 lists in rank order the range of formal public communication activities undertaken by sampled organisations during the year preceding the survey. As a general observation, these results suggest higher levels of formal communication activity than has been indicated by previous studies. For example, 64 percent of Advisory NDPBs claimed to produce annual reports and 18 percent to hold public meetings, compared with figures from the Democratic Audit in 1997 that found only 9 percent of these agencies produced annual reports and 6 percent held public meetings (cited in Weir and Beetham, 1999: 227).

These variations raise the possibility that there has been an increase in quangos' communication activities during the late 1990s, as a consequence of the furore surrounding their public accountability. Significanly, 67 percent of respondents said their publicity and media activities had increased over the previous three years, compared with only 4 percent who said this aspect had reduced. We return to this issue later.

The results in Table 1 also reveal sharp variations across the sector in the extent of public communication activities, with Advisory NDPBs reporting lower levels of publicity activity than executive bodies. Another notable finding is the high proportion of agencies that produced news releases, suggesting the media are a first resort for many quangos in publicity work. Most organisations distributed news releases routinely: 62 percent of organisations distributed at least one news release a month, and 42 percent at least one a week. However, the interviews revealed that the frequency of news release distribution is not a straightforward indicator of their importance as publicity mechanisms. Several senior press officers from organisations with high media profiles said they deliberately used news releases sparingly as a means of enhancing

TABLE 1. Formal Publicity Related Activities/Documents Produced by Quangos over the Preceding Year

	All Sample	Next Step Agency	Exec. NDPB	Advisory NDPB	Tribunals/ Boards of Visitors	NHS Bodies	Housing Associations	HE/FE/City Tech Colleges	GM Schools	TECs/ LECs	Police Authorities	Other local spending bodies*
	%	%	%	%	%	%	%	%	%	%	%	%
Annual Report	88	100	100	64	90	100	87	76	93	96	90	92
News Releases	84	86	79	36	40	94	72	100	89	100	90	92
News-letters	84	86	79	9	10	97	94	95	100	100	90	92
Posters	80	71	79	18	30	100	56	98	70	100	100	96
Adverts	74	71	68	9	20	76	69	93	78	100	80	88
Internet	68	71	89	36	–	73	22	88	67	87	80	88
Exhibi-tions	59	43	63	4	–	88	47	75	44	70	90	69
Confer-ences	59	86	79	18	–	79	31	78	18	87	70	77
Public Meetings	58	29	53	18	20	88	56	44	63	100	90	54
Reports	46	43	98	27	–	62	19	47	11	87	60	58
Briefing Papers	42	29	68	18	–	62	16	47	15	70	70	54
Market Research	38	29	53	4	–	12	22	51	26	78	60	65
News Confer-ences	28	43	53	9	9	43	9	32	–	35	90	28
Number	**274**	7	19	22	10	34	32	59	27	23	10	26

*Career Service Pathfinders, Tourist Boards, Regional Arts Boards.

their effectiveness and took great care to target their distribution, evincing crude "mass mail outs."

MEDIA CONTACT

Although the tailoring of individual news release distribution was often highly context specific–i.e., dependent upon what was being publicised–most interviewees acknowledged that they generally prioritised specialist journals and correspondents, up market newspapers at national level, and local media. These targeting priorities closely mirrored the distribution of actual coverage reported by organisations in the survey.

Only 5 percent of agencies had received no media coverage over the previous year. Of these, 14 agencies were Advisory NDPBs and 3 were

Tribunals or Boards of Visitors. These agency-types were also the ones that reported the lowest levels of contact with mainstream media.

Forty-nine percent of organisations that had received coverage indicated they "generally" or "always" initiated media interactions, compared with 14 percent that "generally" or "always" responded to approaches made by the media. (Thirty-five percent estimated that instances of initiation and response were broadly equal, and 2 percent were unable to judge.) Furthermore, this initiation of contact frequently extended beyond news release distribution. Forty-one percent of quangos said they had informal meetings and contacts with selected journalists. Of these, respondents from Executive NDPBs were most likely to report informal contact (70 percent), followed by Higher Education and Further Education institutions (61 percent), NHS bodies (60 percent), police authorities (60 percent) and TECs/LECs (56 percent). With all other organisational types, no more than 20 percent of responding agencies indicated any informal media contact, with Advisory NDPBs the least likely to report such contact (5 percent).

Most organisations were broadly satisfied with the coverage they received. Seventy two percent that received coverage indicated that they felt it to be "fair" or "very fair," 17 percent were "neutral," and 9 percent felt it "unfair" or "very unfair" (2 percent "didn't know"). In general, complaints centred on the level of coverage rather than its nature: 57 percent said they received "too little," 36 percent "just enough" and 1 percent "too much" (6 percent "didn't know"). Notably, very few organisations said they had occasion to deny journalists' access to information: less than a third said they had ever refused a journalists' request, and most of these instances were to protect individual's rights to privacy, commercial confidentiality or due legal process.

Most organisations seemed well-placed to make informed judgements about the extent and accuracy of their coverage. Eighty-eight percent conducted some form of media monitoring–whether for appraising their own appearances or for general political surveillance–although the interviews revealed wide variations in the sophistication of this work. Again, the agencies least likely to do so were Advisory NDPBs, with less than half conducting any form of monitoring.

BEYOND THE MEDIA: INTENDED AUDIENCES FOR PUBLIC COMMUNICATION

The survey was also used to assess which audiences quangos sought to target through their general publicity work. The most frequently cited target was "The public" (87 percent) followed by "customers/clients" (72 percent), "staff/members" (63 percent), "other professional sources" (56 percent), "local government sources" (51 percent), "business sector sources" (51 percent), "parliamentary sources (42 percent), "voluntary sector sources" (41 percent) and "central government sources" (37 percent).

These results prompt a range of questions. Why is it that specialist audiences are prioritised in news management terms, but lay audiences are most commonly cited as targets for general publicity? Does this mean the news management priorities identified simply reflect a pragmatic identification of the most receptive media arenas, rather than strategic preferences? More generally, does the general prominence of the public contradict the common accusation that in quasi-government "down-line" accountability to the public always comes a poor second to "up line" accountability to government?

To some extent, the prominence of "the public" in this instance is an artefact of the survey categorisation. Whereas "the public" is an imprecise and generic category, the other categories distinguish more precisely between particular political and professional arenas. Once all categories related to professional and political sources were aggregated, 82 percent of agencies cited at least one specialised political or professional arena as a key publicity target.

It is particularly questionable whether these results reveal the dominance of "down line" accountability over "up line" accountability. Firstly, only 38 percent of organisations had conducted any form of public opinion or market research in the previous year (see Table 1), despite government recommendations that quangos should consider using these formal feedback mechanisms more extensively (Cabinet Office, 1998: 11). Such limited systematic citizen consultation contrasts greatly with trends among elected branches of government and political parties in the UK, where citizen polling and focus groups have gained considerable, some would say inordinate, significance in the formulation of policies and political objectives (Ward, 1999). Secondly, when interviewees were asked to identify who they believed their agency was mainly accountable to, government and ministerial sources were the most frequently mentioned (34 percent of all sources referred to in interview). In contrast, references to "the public" or "clients/customers" amounted to 19 percent and 8 percent of cited sources, respectively. Thirdly, these bald statistics alone do not capture the hierarchical nature of accountability described by most interviewees. When discussing accountability to government departments, many interviewees identified its contractual basis and the legal obligations thereby imposed. In contras-, public accountability was described in more abstract terms, often around imprecise and paternalistic notions of public service. In these instances "the public" had a canonical presence, invoked as a broad and imprecise collective that interviewees felt responsible for, rather than beholden to.

Fourthly, it follows that the legal and contractual requirements of "up line accountability" will necessitate the existence of more direct and formal procedures for communication and consultation, i.e. mechanisms for "talking with" external sources, rather than "talking at" them (P.E.R.C, 1996: 2). In this respect, public communication will have a less than central role, but, as we see below, this does not mean it is an irrelevance to government relations.

These points suggest that the issue is not simply which public, professional or political audiences are routinely privileged by quangos in their publicity work, but rather how public communication motives vary in relation to the audiences these agencies seek to address.

PUBLIC COMMUNICATION MOTIVES

When differentiating these motives it is necessary to distinguish between the use of publicity to facilitate scrutiny of organisations' internal operations (*internal accountability*) and its role in aiding organisations' engagement with their external political environment (*external interventions*). It did appear that the political furore surrounding accountability in appointive government had had some recent impact on base line information provision (such as in the production of annual reports and the holding of public meetings). Representatives from most organisations were mindful of the broader debate around accountability, and displayed high levels of awareness in the sector of recent open government recommendations and proposals. But we found little evidence that motives related to *internal accountability* were central to the development of more concerted publicity work. Explanations focused instead on specific matters concerning organisations' *external interventions*.

In noting this, it is also useful to distinguish between external interventions designed to advance the profile and reputation of the agency itself (*organisation promotion*) and those aimed at advancing general issues, practices or values related to an organisation's work (*role promotion*). In specific publicity ventures these motives frequently intertwine, but in the interviewees' comments they were often sharply distinguished, with role promotion concerns being more commonly emphasised than organisation promotion. In part, this seemed to link to the underlying ethos of arms length government, i.e., that it should be characterised by selfless public service and political detachment. In this context, aggressive self-promotion was seen as an anathema. But this does not mean that considerations about organisational promotion were completely absent, rather that their salience varied depending upon which target audiences were being referred to.

Organisational promotion seemed least evident in "down-line" communication to the public, whether through direct publicity campaigns or media contact. In general, the emphasis seemed to be on instructing rather than impressing public opinion. This didactic tendency was also evident in public communication activities aimed at more specialised political and professional audiences, but the more prestigious and influential the target concerned, the more organisation promotion seemed to shade into the equation, particularly in relation to media coverage. Significantly, several interviewees from national organisations mentioned government sources as key targets they sought to address (and impress) through a positive and prominent media presence:

> We have to get over to [ministers] what we do. Because if they are going to have a single regulatory body, they might decide to lump [the agency] back with [another agency] . . . Obviously, at the end of the day it's the Secretary of State that decides, but what I'm trying to say to you is that if we don't get over our messages about what we do and how things have been improved under this system, then we might be disbanded or we might be pushed to one side. (Interviewee, Public Corporation)

In our view, these differences are explained by the specific political characteristics of quasi-governmental bodies. Quangos can afford to be more self-effacing in down line communication because their political authority is not ultimately dependent upon public approval. However, appointed bodies need to be more mindful of their political patrons and other influential opinion leaders in their sphere of activity, as these exert far more direct influence over their political operations and prospects.

Recognising the importance of, on the one hand, conventions of neutrality and, on the other, the *realpolitik* of appointive authority, also explains the privileging of local media, specialist media and (at national level) "up-market" noted earlier. In particular it demonstrates this is more than just a pragmatic identification of the most receptive media environments. Rather, these preferences reveal organisations' acute concerns about having their public interventions trivialised, distorted or sensationalised in media reporting, as this can damage their preferred image as authoritative and dispassionate arbiters in the public policy arena. Therefore, when seeking to communicate with general audiences, these organisations targeted popular media that were recognised as being least likely to distort or disdain their messages. In these respects, the local media were seen to score highly.

The specialist and prestige media sectors were also partly valued for these reasons, but had additional significance because they delivered access to influential political and professional sources whose opinions have greater resonance for many quasi-governmental bodies:

> I want to target the people who read the quality papers . . . It's a way of getting towards MPs, which is obviously important. But in terms of getting those two or three thousand opinion formers, obviously it's more important for me to be in the Times, or the Telegraph, of the FT, before anything else. (Interviewee, Executive NDPB)

THE IMPORTANCE OF PUBLIC COMMUNICATION

From the findings already presented it is evident that the caricature of all quangos' as politically oblivious and pathologically introverted is an oversimplification. However, it would be a mistake to replace one generalisation with another. Whilst the survey suggested structural variations in promotional activities and provision across the sector, the interviews revealed more specific variations in the importance attributed to media and publicity, even among organisations that made substantial investments in these areas. A minority of these interviewees said that media and PR activities tended to be a "bolt on activity" in their organisations' operations, and that their involvement was mainly restricted to the end of any decision-making process. In these agencies, media and publicity personnel were often locked into conventional civil service style hierarchies that restricted their direct access to the most senior echelons of the organisation.

However, in a greater number of instances, interviewees identified public communication considerations as having a core significance for their organisations' operations. In these instances, senior media and publicity officers described an earlier and more direct involvement in high level decision-making and unregulated access to the most senior figures at executive and board level. This high-level access ensured senior publicity officers were informed about all aspects of their organisation's operations, and enabled presentational considerations to feed into the formation of organisational policies and strategies from the outset.

Two factors appeared to create this differential emphasis on public communication matters. As quangos are hierarchical organisations, the disposition and background of senior internal figures have a critical influence on organisations' general media and publicity orientation. Several interviewees claimed a distinct culture change had occurred in their organisation following the appointment of a new head with a more receptive attitude to the media and publicity issues.

But alongside these individual variations, there are evident structural differences across the sector. In a 1995 study, Weir and Hall concluded that Advisory bodies are the most introverted of all quasi-governmental bodies, typically displaying a "mildly hostile attitude towards the idea of opening up their work to public scrutiny and a disdain for the media" (p. 17). Five years on, this judgement seems to retain validity, as these organisations reported consistently less media contact and investment in public communication than other quangos.

This reticence seems to be rooted in several factors. Some advisory agencies only have a finite existence linked to a designated task, which means they will inevitably have less concern about winning and maintaining political legitimacy for their operations than executive agencies whose roles and responsibilities are open-ended and on-going. Additionally, the often confidential nature of their consultations and deliberations can form a barrier against external communication during the earlier stages of their work.

Even where advisory bodies have a developing and ongoing remit, many only convene on an intermittent basis and if they do employ staff, do so on a part-time basis (Weir and Hall, 1995: 6-7). Such conditions are hardly conducive for development of concerted public communication strategies. Added to this, many advisory agencies have narrow or highly technical remits, which will limit their appeal in media terms–particularly when contrasted with executive bodies whose routine decisions often have a wide and material impact upon public life. Finally, the recalcitrance of advisory bodies may in part reflect that they "are officially seen as outside the need for accountability because they merely advise" (P.E.R.C, 1996: 4). However, some see this as dangerously complacent assumption, as it underestimates the significant influence this formative input can have on the public policy arena. For instance, in Weir and Beetham's comprehensive democratic audit of the British political system, the role of advisory bodies is identified as "at least as important, and possibly more so, than that of executive quangos" (1999: 219).

CONTROL AND AUTONOMY

A recurrent accusation levelled against quangos is that they have little meaningful independence from government and that their vaunted "arms length" relationship is just a means for enacting government policy by stealth. Certainly, if the most conspiratorial versions of these claims are correct (e.g., Cook, 1995, chapter 2) one would expect to find high levels of government intervention in quangos' publicity and media activity–particularly given the growing promotional sensibilities of the British state (Deacon and Golding, 1994) which have become even more attuned over the recent period (Franklin, 1999).

An interesting perspective on this matter is offered by Nicholas Jones, a senior political reporter with the BBC. No stranger to robust official news management, Jones remarks in the concluding chapter of his book *Soundbites and Spin Doctors*:

> Civil servants have managed over the years to achieve a considerable degree of co-ordination in the flow of newsworthy material from the state. While their efforts have never satisfied their political masters, they currently face greater organisational challenges than in the past . . . New sources of information have opened up through the increasing dispersal of public services to "arms length" agencies which often have their own procedures for dealing with the news media. (1995: 222)

This offers a different viewpoint from the one commonly paraded in discussions about government patronage, as it claims that the proliferation of quangos has compromised rather than consolidated the capacity of the government to command the terms of public policy presentation. Contained within it is the proposition that arms length agencies enjoy considerable freedom of operation in publicity work.

To assess the legitimacy of this claim, survey respondents were asked to indicate the frequency with which various internal and external sources had a direct involvement in the *production* of publicity material by their agency and/or were given advance notice of publicity content (*consultation*) (see Table 2).

TABLE 2. Extent of Internal and External Sources' Involvement in "Quangos" Publicity Work

	Involvement in the Production of Publicity Material (Internal and External Sources)			
	Always	Quite Often	Sometimes	Never
	%	%	%	%
In House Press and Publicity Staff	59	15	1	25
Head of Quango	26	25	41	8
Other Quango Staff	12	29	34	25
External Press/PR	5	6	17	72
Govt Ministers	3	4	23	70
Other Central Govt Sources	2	2	21	76
Other	5	2	3	95
	Prior Consultation Over Publicity Material? (External Sources Only)			
	Always	Quite Often	Sometimes	Never
Other Central Government Sources	8	9	34	49
Govt Ministers	8	5	30	56
Other Staff	8	11	21	60
Local Govt	5	8	34	53
Other Public Sector	3	10	37	50
Parliamentary Sources	3	4	22	71
General Public	3	6	18	72
Voluntary Sector	1	6	34	59
Other Sources	1	2	3	94

Internal Sources: "Routine Matters" and "High Level Stuff"

The results highlight the primary involvement of internal sources in the production of publicity material, with, predictably, in-house media and publicity staff at the forefront. Senior figures also feature prominently, but the fact that their involvement is not as regular as designated media and publicity staff, suggests some internal devolution of responsibilities. To assess the boundaries of this freedom, the internal arrangements governing media relations were analysed in detail in the interviews.

Some variation was evident across these organisations in the degree of autonomy media and publicity personnel were permitted. Some were required to clear everything through senior board or executive figures, but more were licensed to exercise their own judgement about the permission required for particular media interactions. In these cases, senior approval was only sought when issues touched upon broader policy matters connected with an agency's work, government policy and relations, or some issue of public controversy.

Media and publicity personnel also described varying levels of control over other members of staff concerning media contact. In most organisations, the press office was the fulcrum of a high control culture, typified by a remark from a senior press officer from a national executive NDPB that "No one can speak to the media without the express permission of this office. It doesn't matter how senior they are, other than the Chief Executive." But this centralisation was not universal. Some organisations had more relaxed arrangements and condoned some contact between media and other staff without their prior involvement. At national level, this was most evident with organisations that had regional branches and staff, and where completely centralised control was deemed impracticable.

Strict protocols governing media contact were in part defensive mechanisms designed to prevent damage to the reputation of an agency through ill judged or inadvertent comment. However, controls were also intended to facilitate media access, by routing journalistic enquiries to staff with the necessary authority and expertise to comment, and advising staff how to present information to the media in an effective way.

EXTERNAL CONTROL:
"A POLICY OF NO SURPRISES"

The results in Table 2 also appear to demonstrate that external sources rarely have any direct input into the production of quangos' publicity material, and are infrequently given advance notice of any public announcement. In particular, the irregularity with which government sources are consulted suggests that whatever obligations quangos may feel in relation to up-line accountability, there is little sign of a clearance mentality in their external communication work. However, these statistics only reveal the regularity of governmental involvement, not the conditions under which it can or does occur. In the interviews we sought to clarify when quangos might refer publicity matters to government and ministers, and how far they would brook intervention from these sources.

Although most interviewees saw operational independence from government in this area as a cornerstone of their political legitimacy, most conceded they were mindful of government in their publicity affairs and engaged in some consultation on sensitive topics. This sensitivity was most acute among national agencies, because of their greater sphere of operations, higher national profile and geographical proximity to Whitehall. Not surprisingly, Next Step Agencies revealed the closest departmental links and the least discretion in their media and publicity work, as they remain part of their sponsoring department.

The kind of "up line" consultation most consistently described was characterised by one interviewee as "a policy of no surprises"–a process of notifying government of their intentions rather than seeking permission to proceed.

Most agencies that had close links with government described them as co-operative and non-conflictive, although a couple of interviewees described persistently tense and fraught relations, relating to long standing "turf wars" between their organisations and linked government departments regarding the appropriate administrative and political responsibilities of each. These broader political tensions often created disputes over publicity matters.

These cases aside, the picture suggested by both the survey and interviews corroborates Jones's remarks about the day to day operational autonomy of most arms length agencies in their communication activities. But it does not follow that the government exerts no routine influence over the communication activities of quangos. One obvious mechanism is the regular, high level interactions between quango-leaders and senior government sources. Given the hierarchical nature of quangos, it follows that if the leader is kept on-side, whether through negotiation, persuasion or coercion, then the agency will follow. Furthermore, there is the long-term, strategic influence government can exert through the definition of quangos' remits and its involvement the appointment of senior personnel.

We highlight these factors not to deny the claims made by quango representatives about their room for independent action from government, but rather to emphasise that this freedom amounts to a "licensed autonomy." This phrase was first coined by Curran (1990) to describe the limited freedom of editors and journalists from direct intervention from proprietors, but it also encapsulates the power relations that pertain between quangos and government.

CONCLUDING REMARKS

This examination of the communication activities of quasi-governmental bodies and their media relations shows that claims about the insularity of these organisations have been overstated. Many quangos recognise media and publicity as integral to their operations and invest considerable resources in these areas. However, variation is evident across the sector, reflecting individual and structural factors: notably, the disposition of quango-chiefs and differences in organisations' functions and funding. As a general trend, quangos with extensive, open-ended, executive remits have the most developed public communication strategies and media profiles, and organisations with narrow, finite and advisory functions, have the least.

Most quangos have some independence in organising their public communication. However, this amounts to tactical autonomy, rather than absolute freedom. Government influence, in particular, tends to be exerted strategically and in the long term, through the designation of quangos' roles and the appointment of senior personnel. Additionally, some agencies are permitted more discretion than others in their publicity work, reflecting the different structural relations between particular types of quangos and central government.

In the main, quangos' public communication strategies exist to facilitate (and promote) their political functions, not to encourage scrutiny of their internal workings. This is not necessarily for sinister reasons, neither is this strategic emphasis unique to these organisations. (Presenting a positive profile to the outside world while protecting access on private matters, can be said to be defining features of all public relations work.) But it is important to appreciate that if the findings presented here challenge glib over-generalisations about quangos' introversion, they do not assuage ongoing concerns about openness and public accountability in the sector.

More generally, the notable, if uneven, emphasis on public communication in the quasi-governmental sector may be symptomatic of a general spread of "promotionalism" across political and institutional cultures, but it displays certain unique characteristics. There is far less evidence of the populist imperative that is affecting political communication in the electoral domain. Although many agencies recognised a paternalistic responsibility to communicate with the public, they seemed less concerned about courting public opinion. In contrast, concerns about impression management and self-promotion were more evident in "up-line" and (to some extent) "sideways" communication. This pattern seems to reflect the particular nature and status of quasi-governmental organisations. As non-elected bodies, they are considerably (but not completely) insulated from the power of public opinion. However, as appointed bodies, quangos need to demonstrate their effectiveness to their patrons, at the same time as convincing other influential opinion-leaders of their operational independence and effectiveness. High levels of positive coverage in prestigious media sectors assist both these objectives.

The fact that most quangos can foster their media links far more selectively than elected bodies–whether with specialist or prestige media, that are less concerned about audience maximisation and less inclined to sensationalism, or with local or popular entertainment media, that are not renowned for their critical abrasiveness–not only makes for far less conflictive media relations than are evident in the electoral sphere, but alerts us to the fact that within a changing political environment, "communications dependency" (Blumler and Gurevitch, 1996) is a relative matter.

NOTE

1. The paper is based on a research project funded by the Economic and Social Research Council (Grant Reference: R000236953).

BIBLIOGRAPHY

Blumler, J. and Gurevitch, M. (1996). "Media Change and Social Change: Linkages and Junctures." In Curran, J. and Gurevitch, M. (eds.), *Mass Media and Society* (Second Edition) London: Edward Arnold.
Cabinet Office. (1998). *Quangos: Opening the Doors*, London: HMSO.
Cabinet Office. (1999). *Statistical Summary: Non-Departmental Public Bodies 1979-1998*, London: HMSO.
Cook, J. (1995). *The Sleaze File . . . and How to Clean up British Politics*, London: Bloomsbury.
Curran, J. (1990). "Culturalist Perspectives of News Organisations: A Reappraisal and a Case Study." In Ferguson, M. (ed.), *Public Communication: The New Imperatives*, London: Sage.
Davis, H. (1996). "Quangos and Local Government: A Changing World." In Davis, H. (ed.), (1996) *Quangos and Local Government: A Changing World*, London: Frank Cass.
Deacon, D. and Monk, P. (2000). "Executive Stressed? News Reporting of Quangos in Britain." *Press and Politics*, 53.
Downing, J. (1986). "Government secrecy and the media in the United States and Britain." In P. Golding, G. Murdoch and P. Schlesinger (eds.), *Communicating Politics: Mass Communication and the Political Process*, Leicester: Leicester University Press.
Franklin, B. (ed). (1999). *Social Policy, the Media and Misrepresentation*, London: Routledge.

Gay, O. (1996). *The Quango Debate*, Research Paper 96/72, Home Affairs Section, London: HMSO.

Jones, N. (1995). *Soundbites and Spin Doctors: How Politicians Manipulate the Media and Vice Versa*, London: Cassell.

Marr, A. (1995). *Ruling Britannia: The Failure of British Democracy*, London: Penguin.

Mazzolena, G. and Schultz, W. (1999). " 'Mediatization' of politics: A Challenge for Democracy?," *Political Communication*, 16: 247-261.

Negrine, R. (1996). *The Communication of Politics*, London: Sage.

P.E.R.C. (Political Economy Research Council). (1996). *Quangos: Why Governments Love Them*, Sheffield: PERC, University of Sheffield.

Ske cher, C. (1998). *The Appointed State: Quasi-Governmental Organizations and Democracy*, Milton Keynes: Open University Press.

Ward, L. (1999). "Ministers Spending Millions on Secret Polls," *Guardian*, 3 Sept: 1.

Weir, S. & Hall, W. (1996). *The Untouchables*, London: Democratic Audit/Scarman Trust.

Weir, S. and Beetham, D. (1999). *Political Power and Democratic Control in Britain*, London: Routledge.

Weir, S. and Hall, W. (1995). *Behind Closed Doors*, Democratic Audit Paper No. 4, Essex: Human Rights Centre, University of Essex.

Wernick, A. (1991). *Promotional Culture: Advertising, Ideology and Symbolic Expression*. London: Sage.

Whitehead, A. (1995). *Holding Quangos to Account*. Local Government Information Unit Discussion Papers/Reforming the Quango State, London: LGIU.

New Labour:
A Study of the Creation, Development
and Demise of a Political Brand

Jon White
Leslie de Chernatony

Birmington University Business School, UK

SUMMARY. This paper examines the use made by political parties of branding, as a means of establishing party values and winning political support. It looks in particular at the way in which political parties use communication to create, build and maintain political brands.

The paper involves an examination of the recent history of the British Labour Party. After a long period in the political wilderness, the party re-branded itself as "New Labour" in the mid-1990s, and–as New Labour– swept to power in a landslide election victory in 1997, under their new leader, Tony Blair.

Using media coverage and material written by some of the architects of New Labour, the paper will describe the creation of the "New Labour" brand, and look at how it was developed and used to generate political sup-

Jon White is Associate at the Henley Management College and Honorary Professor of Public Affairs at Birmingham University Business School, University of Birmingham.

Leslie de Chernatony is Professor of Brand Marketing at Birmingham University Business School, University of Birmingham.

[Haworth co-indexing entry note]: "New Labour: A Study of the Creation, Development and Demise of a Political Brand." White, Jon, and Leslie de Chernatony. Co-published simultaneously in *Journal of Political Marketing* (The Haworth Political Press, an imprint of The Haworth Press, Inc.) Vol. 1, No. 2/3, 2002, pp. 45-52; and: *Communication of Politics: Cross-Cultural Theory Building in the Practice of Public Relations and Political Marketing* (eds: Bruce I. Newman, and Dejan Verčič) The Haworth Political Press, an imprint of The Haworth Press, Inc., 2002, pp. 45-52. Single or multiple copies of this article are available for a fee from The Haworth Document Delivery Service [1-800-HAWORTH, 9:00 a.m. - 5:00 p.m. (EST). E-mail address: getinfo@haworthpressinc.com].

10.1300/J199v01n02_04

port. The paper will also consider the evolution and development of the brand, as the substance underlying the stated brand values has come to be questioned, not least by so-called "Old Labour" supporters of the party.

The paper will draw conclusions regarding the successful management of a political brand, pointing in particular at the need to ensure that the performance of a party espousing a particular brand supports and reinforces communicated brand values and the brand itself. *[Article copies available for a fee from The Haworth Document Delivery Service: 1-800-HAWORTH. E-mail address: <getinfo@haworthpressinc.com> Website: <http://www.HaworthPress.com> © 2002 by The Haworth Press, Inc. All rights reserved.]*

KEYWORDS. New Labour, political branding, political parties, Tony Blair, United Kingdom

INTRODUCTION

Political parties emerge as a response to social developments, when groups of people feel that they have an approach to social questions around which they wish to gather support, or which they seek to defend and promote in the face of opposition. Political parties have histories, traditions and approaches to managing their own affairs. They also acquire and use names and symbols, to strengthen their own positions, to rally their supporters, to garner further support and, perhaps, to intimidate their opponents.

In recent years, political parties have turned to techniques of marketing to manage their affairs and further their interests. Since World War II, and drawing to a large extent on the experience of political parties in the United States and other developed democracies, political parties in North America and Europe, and more recently in emerging democracies such as South Africa and the countries of central and Eastern Europe, have made steadily increasing use of these techniques.

This paper looks in particular at the use of branding by political parties, and at the recent experience of the United Kingdom's Labour Party which put branding at the heart of the process of modernization which led to the party's return to power–after a long absence–in the country's general election of 1997. Since then, and using the same techniques, the party has consolidated its hold on power in an election held in June 2001.

The paper examines the creation of the "New Labour" brand, looking at how it was developed and used to generate political support. The paper will also consider the evolution and development of the brand, as the substance underlying the stated brand values has come to be questioned, not least by so-called "Old Labour" supporters of the party.

The paper also considers the successful management of a political brand, pointing in particular at the need to ensure that the performance of a party espousing a particular brand supports and reinforces communicated brand values and the brand itself. Throughout, the importance of communication in establishing and sustaining the brand cannot be understated.

BRANDING

A brand is a multidimensional construct, involving the blending of functional and emotional values to match consumers' performance and psychosocial needs (de Chernatony and Dall'Olmo Riley, 1998). One of the goals of branding is to make a brand unique on dimensions that are both relevant and welcomed by consumers (de Chernatony and McDonald, 1998).

Success in an overcrowded market will depend on effective brand differentiation, based on the identification, internalization and communication of unique brand values that are both pertinent to and desired by consumers.

Powerful brands communicate their values through every point of contact they have with consumers (Cleaver, 1999).

A functional value is a value relating to the way something works or operates and can be evaluated through rational deduction. An emotional value is a value relating to a person's emotions and derived from a person's circumstances, mood or relationships with others, and being instinctive or intuitive or based on feelings, as distinguished from reasoning or knowledge.

APPLYING BRANDING PRINCIPLES TO A POLITICAL PARTY– THE CASE OF NEW LABOUR

A political party, despite the difficulty of defining the market place for its brand, can consider itself as a brand, to be developed to offer functional and emotional values to an electorate as part of its appeal.

The New Labour brand was developed as part of the modernisation of the Labour party, which occurred of necessity between 1983 and 1994. By the 1983 election, the Labour party's support had reduced to the point where there was a danger it might lose its position as official opposition to the increasingly powerful and secure Conservative Party. The Conservative Party had come to power in 1979, replacing a weak and failing Labour government. It was to remain in power until 1997, through elections in 1983, 1987 and 1992. By 1983, the Conservative Party was making strong use of marketing techniques to sustain its hold on power (White, 1983).

"New Labour was the product of traumatic and multiple failures" (Rawnsley, 2000, page viii). It emerged from recognition through three election defeats, that the party had to modernize, reconnect to the electorate, and overcome the electorate's doubts and fears about Labour as a party of government. The process of modernization is well-described in books such as Gould, 1998. He first mooted the term "New Labour" in 1989, but the term and the brand were not adopted until the 1994 Party Conference, which had the theme, New Labour, New Britain.

The New Labour brand represented an explicit break with "Old Labour," the party of tradition and the almost one hundred years of history that the party had lived through since its foundation as a party to represent the interests of organized Labour.

New Labour had to break explicitly with the past, and to demonstrate the new party's commitment to current values. This involved changing the party's constitution and founding principles, among them Clause IV, which committed the party to taking significant components of the economy into public ownership. A revised Clause IV allowed for the workings of the market economy.

New Labour set out to represent functional values of openness, modernity, economic orthodoxy and redistributory social policy. Emotionally, the brand had to reassure, remove the fear that voters still after many years felt that a Labour government would return the country to the dark days of the "winter of discontent," when the country was paralyzed by union disputes in the winter of 1978-1979, under the last Labour government.

Labour set out to appeal to middle England, recognizing it is most successful as a party when it bestrides the centre ground (*The Economist*, November 15, 1997).

THE EVOLUTION AND DEVELOPMENT OF THE BRAND

Improvement of the Labour product and the communication of its benefits went hand in hand (Fletcher, in *Marketing*, November 27,

1997). Gould (1998) shows how, partly as a result of his experiences with the US presidential campaign in 1992, he and other advisors were able to professionalise the process of party and campaign communication through the elections of 1987 and 1992, and in the successful election of 1997. Gould, a strategy and polling advisor to Tony Blair and the Labour Party in the 1997 General Election campaign and in the three years that preceded it, is one of the central figures in the modernization of the the the Labour Party, but the architects of New Labour are recognized as Tony Blair (now Prime Minister), Gordon Brown (Chancellor of the Exchequer), Alastair Campbell (the Prime Minister's press secretary) and Peter Mandelson (a close advisor to the Prime Minister, and recognized master of communication techniques used in the pursuit and retention of political power).

In the 1997 election, Labour came to power with 419 seats in the House of Commons, for a majority of 179. The Conservatives retained 165 seats.

New Labour as a brand was successful in part because of its ambiguity. It represented values with which large swathes of the population could identify, such as personal opportunity flowing out of strong communities. It was an easy target for criticism. *The Economist*, for example, said that Tony Blair's project to establish New Labour in government was to achieve cultural hegemony by creating a more inclusive politics for a post ideological age (*The Economist*, October 25, 1997).

Rawnsley (2000) talked about the illusions that sustained New Labour. He said "the illusionists are best placed to know what an illusion it was that New Labour was a glossily impotent machine always under the masterful control of an assured leader. That this illusion was maintained for so long was one of the great triumphs of Alastair Campbell's spin."

THE DEMISE OF THE BRAND

New Labour was described by Derek Draper, an aide to Peter Mandelson in the 1997 campaign, as "an election strategy rather than a governing strategy" in comments to a forum to assess New Labour's record held in 2001, at London's Institute for Contemporary Arts.

Nevertheless, Tony Blair, speaking outside his office at Number 10 Downing Street on May 2, the day following the election in 1997, said "we ran for office as New Labour and will govern as New Labour. It will be a government that seeks to restore trust in politics" (speech in Downing Street, May 2, 1997, quoted in Rawnsley, 2000, p. 15).

However, Philip Gould, writing in a memo to the party leadership in May 2000, Getting the Right Place in History, said by then the New Labour brand has "been badly contaminated. It is the object of constant criticism and, even worse, ridicule . . . Labour is undermined by a combination of spin, lack of conviction and apparent lack of integrity" (Gibbon, 2000).

Part of the contamination was due to the discrepancy between the high aspirations incorporated into the brand's values, and the performance of the party in office. In an end of term assessment, Toynbee and Walker (2001) wrote "expectations had been raised, only to be dashed when nothing much happened, or with transport, things evidently got worse. Early trickery with figures undermined confidence" (Toynbee and Walker, 2001, page 230).

Other commentators felt that it was hard to find much that was concrete, let alone distinct and consistent, in the principles on which New Labour's approach was built (*The Economist*, May 2, 1998; White, 1999). The article concluded that it would be better to judge New Labour by its deeds rather than by its words.

The New Labour government embarked upon its first years in office on a flurry of activity, but early on attracted criticism for the tightness of control it sought to maintain on information, and on the messages delivered by government and the people who spoke for it. Charges of "control freakery" and "spin" were directed against the government.

Marketing professionals asked if New Labour had spun totally out of control (*Marketing*, July 27, 2000). In mid-2000, as the government seemed to lurch from one crisis to another (for example, the fuel crisis of September, 2000) the New Labour brand was seen to be under threat. The brand was discredited by internal disputes within the party, and a perceived inability on the part of the government to take control of current issues. Where the brand once stood for modernity, integrity and competence, it now seemed to represent elitism, spin and drift.

Toynbee and Walker's assessment of the government's record prior to the 2001 election, at which Labour was returned to office with a comparable majority concluded that the government was "a modest, competent, unambitious government, over-given to high flown rhetoric while trimming its sails to every wind" (Toynbee and Walker, 2001, page 239).

From mid-2000, use of the term "New Labour" lessened. One report at about this time suggested that the term new was now redundant (*Daily Telegraph*, July 20, 2000).

CONCLUSIONS

Reflections on the emergence, development, evolution and demise of the New Labour brand suggest a number of conclusions. The brand was an essential element in the modernization of the party, and a device to suggest and promise changes. The brand promise, vague though it seemed to commentators at the time, was aimed to reassure, to allay fears and to convince the electorate that Labour would provide a new kind of government.

The brand came to be devalued when some of the important promises made were not delivered. One of these had to do with the standards to be followed by the government in the conduct of public business, but early illustrations of government and ministerial performance showed that the government was essentially no different from other governments (Rawnsley 2000, see in particular the Ecclestone affair, and the forced resignation of Peter Mandelson from ministerial posts).

The brand was built through communication (Gould, 1998), but the discrepancies between announcements and actual performance led on to cynicism about the government, New Labour and politics itself. This cynicism led on to poor voter turnout at the 2001 election.

REFERENCES

Cleaver, C., 1999. Brands as the Catalyst. *The Journal of Brand Management* 6, 309-312.

De Chernatony, L., 2001. From Brand Vision to Brand Evaluation: Strategically Building and Sustaining Brands. Oxford, Butterworth-Heinemann.

De Chernatony, L. & McDonald, M., 1999. Creating Powerful Brands in Consumer, Service and Industrial Markets. Oxford, Butterworth-Heinemann.

De Chernatony, L., & Dall'Olmo Riley, F., 1998. Defining A "Brand": Beyond The Literature With Experts' Interpretations. *Journal of Marketing Management*, 14, 417-443.

Fletcher, W., 1997. New Labour can show marketers how job's done. *Marketing*, November 27.

Gibbon, G., 2000. New Leak Rocks Labour, Channel 4 News Special Report (broadcast, July 19, 2000).

Gould, P., 1998. The Unfinished Revolution: How the Modernisers Saved the Labour Party. Little Brown and Company (UK), London.

Has New Labour Spun Totally Out of Control. *Marketing*, London, July 27, 2000.

King, A., 1997. New Labour Triumphs: Britain at the Polls, Chatham House, London.

Labour's First Year: The Long Honeymoon. *The Economist*, May 2, 1998

New Labour, New History. *The Economist*, November 15, 1997.

New Labour, New Language. *The Economist*, October 25, 1997.

Rawnsley, A., 2000. Servants of the People: The Inside Story of New Labour. Hamish Hamilton, London.

Toynbee, P., & Walker, D., 2001. Did Things Get Better? An Audit of Labour's Successes and Failures. Penguin Books, London.

White, J., 1983. There Was No Alternative: Implications of the Parties' Public Relations Approaches in the 1983 General Election Campaign. *Public Relations (International Journal of the Institute of Public Relations)*. Autumn, Vol. 2, No. 1, pp. 26-27.

White, S., 1999. Which Way?: The Third Way and the Puzzle of New Labour. *Harvard International Review*, Vo. 21, pp. 54-59.

Political Marketing Research in the 2000 U.S. Election

Elaine Sherman

Hofstra University, USA

Leon G. Schiffman

St. John's University, USA

SUMMARY. It is not news that polls and other forms of marketing research are regularly employed to craft political strategy. What is new is that the 2000 U.S. election represented a turning point where political marketing research seems to take center stage. The print and broadcast media employed polls and other forms of research at levels far beyond anything ever seen before. At times, it appeared as if almost as much attention was being given to polls as was being given to the political candidates and the issues. This was clearly a new and important posturing of the role of political marketing research. With this as a backdrop, the current article compares polls and other forms of political research–focusing on what went wrong and what was right in terms of the use of polls, focus groups and Internet re-

Elaine Sherman is Professor of Marketing at Hofstra University, Zarb School of Business, 224 Weller Hall, Hempstead, NY 11549 (E:mail: mktezs@hofstra.edu).

Leon G. Schiffman is Professor of Marketing and J. Donald Kennedy Endowed Chair in E-Commerce at St. John's University, Peter J. Tobin College of Business, 8000 Utopia Parkway, Jamaica, NY 11439 (E-mail: SchiffmanL@aol.com).

Parts of this article were drawn from the authors' PowerPoint presentation delivered at the Symposium of Public Relations Research, held in Slovenia, July 7, 2001.

[Haworth co-indexing entry note]: "Political Marketing Research in the 2000 U.S. Election." Sherman, Elaine, and Leon G. Schiffman. Co-published simultaneously in *Journal of Political Marketing* (The Haworth Political Press, an imprint of The Haworth Press, Inc.) Vol. 1, No. 2/3, 2002, pp. 53-68; and: *Communication of Politics: Cross-Cultural Theory Building in the Practice of Public Relations and Political Marketing* (eds: Bruce I. Newman, and Dejan Verčič) The Haworth Political Press, an imprint of The Haworth Press, Inc., 2002, pp. 53-68. Single or multiple copies of this article are available for a fee from The Haworth Document Delivery Service [1-800-HAWORTH, 9:00 a.m. - 5:00 p.m. (EST). E-mail address: getinfo@haworthpressinc.com].

10.1300/J199v01n02_05

search during the 2000 U.S. election. The article ends with the presentation of some exploratory research that examines insights about respondents' opinions regarding the impact of political polls. *[Article copies available for a fee from The Haworth Document Delivery Service: 1-800-HAWORTH. E-mail address: <getinfo@haworthpressinc.com> Website: <http://www.HaworthPress.com> © 2002 by The Haworth Press, Inc. All rights reserved.]*

KEYWORDS. Political marketing research, political strategy, 2000 U.S. election, political polls, focus group and Internet research opinions on the impact of political polls

INTRODUCTION

While previous elections have seen the frequent use of polls and other standard marketing research tools to formulate political strategy, the 2000 U.S. election was a watershed election in that it witnessed political marketing research taking center stage. In particular, the news media employed polls and other political marketing research methodologies at levels far beyond anything ever seen before. Moreover, in general, the 2000 presidential election shattered all records for the most polls ever taken for such an election. According to *USA Today,* in the first seven months of 2000 the news media carried out more than five times the number of polls than they did 20 years earlier–in 1980 (Benedello and Drinkard, 2000). It has been suggested that interest in polls has become as pronounced as the political candidates and their messages (Steinhorn and Carroll, 2000).

The rapid growth in political research has lead critics of the political process to suggest that "political reporting increasingly resembles sports coverage, with endless polls telling who is gaining ground" (Buell, 2001). In such an environment, major news media, political candidates, current officeholders, and an endless variety of special interest groups are continuously bombarding citizens with polling results to help give them "the facts." In addition, major TV and cable news networks are now regularly conducting and presenting their own focus group sessions. These group sessions are being presented realtime; thus, allowing the citizen-viewers to "look-in" on the process as it is occurring. To all this, add the rapid growth in the use and popularity of dial-in and Internet surveys.

Given this setting, it is our objective to first set the stage about political marketing research, by examining the following issues: (1) polls and how they differ from other forms of political marketing research, (2) what went wrong in the use of polls in the 2000 U.S. election (especially on election night), (3) the strengths and emerging opportunities in using political polling, (4) the "public good" of political polls, (5) the increasing popularity of qualitative research methods as part of political marketing research, (6) the emergence of the Internet as a political research methodology and content outlet, and (7) the voting public's expectation for political polls. Following our consideration of political polling and other forms of political marketing research in the 2000 U.S. election, we will consider the findings of our exploratory research that was undertaken in order to expand our understanding of respondents' opinions regarding polls, the role of polling, and their perceived impact on voters ("themselves" and "others") and politicians.

DISTINGUISHING POLLS FROM OTHER FORMS OF POLITICAL MARKETING RESEARCH

To set the stage for our discussion of political marketing research, it is useful for us to briefly distinguish between the make-up of political polls and other forms of political marketing research. Political polls can be thought of as a form of research that is designed to gauge potential voters' intentions with respect to voting or acting in a particular way with respect to a candidate, an election, or a political issue. It is also useful to think of polls as primarily focused on the measurement of voters' or citizens' attitudes or opinions, preferences, or potential actions with respect to political candidates or issues. While not always the case, it is our view that polls should be distinguished from other forms of surveys, focus groups or depth interviews. Most often these other research formats are employed to measure a wider range and complexity of political issues, or even to develop or test selected hypotheses.

While polling appears to be simple ("deceptively simple"), in reality polling is a demanding and complex combination of "art and science." Question wording and ordering, and response rates and patterns are difficult to control. Polls are always subject to who is home and who is likely to answer the telephone at the time of a poll. Political polls are also subject to a wide range situational issues–e.g., the closeness of the race, the closeness to the actual election day, and the need to often meet unrealistic news deadlines. All these contextual factors influence the quality and accuracy of the insights secured from polls. While expert pollsters have an experience-base to drawn upon to deal with some of these challenges; nevertheless, at the end of the day, there is a lot of room for errors and mishaps.

Still further, with a large and diverse potential voting population to choose from, it is often an extremely demanding task to select an appropriate or representative sample of Americans to poll. Adding to the challenge is the reality that many polls must account for a mixture of national, regional, state, and local elections. This often means that by the time election day rolls around there is excessive pressure to get the results of exit polls in the hands of the news media to present to their audiences. In the midst of such a rushed atmosphere, it is too easy to forget about the challenges of dealing with time zone differences that plague national and even some regional level elections. The reality of time zone differences means that while elections may be over in one state or region, they may still be ongoing in other states or regions. Still further, if we are considering a particularly close race (as it was in the 2000 U.S. presidential election), it is especially difficult to call the final election outcome.

Available research also indicates that voters who favor a political candidate are more likely to expect the candidate to win the election (Babad and Yacabos, 1993). This implies that a portion of voters tend to overestimate the likelihood that their preferred candidates will win the election. Given such an effect, we might expect that a line of questioning that asks a potential voter who will win a particular election might produce false or misleading results (Morwitz and Pluzinski, 1996). To overcome some of these difficulties, the media and politicians are increasingly employing *tracking polls* to gauge voter views or preferences over time. One outgrowth of the 2000 U.S. election was that the major U.S. TV networks promised the U.S. Congress that they will change the way they cover elections in the future (Borger, 2001).

Adding to the "mess" of predicting the outcome of a political race is the large number of potential American voters who are either "apathetic" or "undecided" (Chin, 2001). The impact of these potentially election-making voters often remain a "mystery" up until the time of the actual vote counting. Before the election, their opinions and possible actions can fluctuate greatly, producing swings in survey results. For instance, in a specific pre-election poll–e.g., with a sample of registered voters–the "margin of error" can vary in either direction by a set number of percentage points. Add to this an uncertain polling climate (e.g., a close race, with many undecided voters), and it become relatively easy to miscall the results of a particular election (Harwood and Crossen, 2000).

SKEPTICISM ABOUT POLITICAL POLLING DURING THE 2000 U.S. PRESIDENTIAL ELECTION

Ironically, despite all the polling experience acquired by the news media, the 2000 U.S. election night was a *polling fiasco*. The early election results were wrong and misleading. The news media first predicted that Al Gore was going to be the winner, and then they reversed their prediction and declared that George W. Bush had won Florida and that he was going to win the election. They showed a "narrow and herdlike" mentality, one which drew sharp criticism and lowered their credibility with viewers (Buell, 2001).

Network news organizations ultimately claimed that the inaccurate results were caused by undue haste (pressure to get the results on air) and the over-reliance on a single exit-polling organization's results. Specifically, all of the major TV news networks based their predictions on data supplied by the Voter News Service. This single exit-polling consortium was established by the TV networks to conduct exit-polls and gather results from a sample of electoral precincts. The exit-polling consortium was created by the TV networks in order to save money. The TV networks were already spending astronomical sums of money on broadcasting the election night results of the presidential, state and local political races. They mistakenly thought that they could cut corners and still be accurate in their early forecasts–again, the decision was a complete fiasco. In effect by "joining forces," they effectively eliminated any opportunity to identify any discrepancies, and the problem went undetected. The outcome was that all the news media made the wrong prediction, and were ultimately embarrassed by their blunder. Moreover, they may have seriously harmed the election by reporting outcomes of East coast elections, while West coast voting was still ongoing. These problems point-up some of the potentially serious consequences of inappropriate administration of polls, without adequate safeguards.

In various countries throughout world, the publication of poll results immediately before an election is frowned upon or is even illegal. Some of the critics argue that the very frequent reporting of polls contributes to the deterioration of the overall quality of political investigative reporting. In particular, they suggest that quickly generated short polls are replacing lengthy in-depth research articles (Pobst, 1999). Moreover, there is the view that polls distort actual political outcomes, by creating a misguided "bandwagon effect"–that is, encouraging potential voters to vote for the *most popular candidate* (in terms of poll results) instead of the *best candidate* (Newman, 1984). In addition, if a candidate is the frontrunner, he/she will be perceived as a winner and receive more press coverage, while the perceived "loser" is viewed negatively and generally receive less media attention (Benedetto and Drinkard, 2000).

SOME ADVANCES IN POLITICAL POLLING AND MARKETING RESEARCH

Not all was negative in applying marketing research methodologies in the 2000 U.S. election. Political candidates used a variety of newer techniques to attempt to more effectively target narrower segments of the overall voting population. For example, lifestyle or psychographic clustering was increasingly used to profile specific voter segments; and politicians were becoming adept at identifying and courting the important "swing voters" (Teachout, 2001). There was also increased emphasis on examining "hybrid voter segments," composed of elaborate combinations of U.S. census demographic analysis and geodemographic segmentation analysis. These refined methodologies have been praised for their ability to indicate variations in voting patterns.

THE "PUBLIC GOOD" OF POLITICAL POLLS

Some hail political polls as a valuable source of insights–reflecting public opinion and aiding politicians in their task of understanding the views of the voting public. For this group of poll users, polls are indispensable for crafting campaign strategy and targeting voters, or as information to assist in the task of allocating campaign resources and funds (Pobst, 1999). Polls have also been seen as providing input for political analysis, and they allow politicians to be more sensitive to the needs of their constituents. Gallup maintains that polls are tools for deciphering public sentiment and enabling policy makers to respond to what their constituents want (Jacobs and Shapiro, 1995-1996).

Others stress that poll results provide information that enables potential voters to gauge the sentiment of fellow citizens on a wide range of issues. This point-of-view supports the idea that the presentation of poll results make for a more informed voting public, one which is in a better position to make more informed decisions (Newman, 1994; Katz, 2001). Within this context, public opinion polls perform a valuable informational service by providing potential voters with the opportunity of learning what their fellow citizens are thinking with regard to the issues or candidates.

THE APPEAL OF POLITICAL QUALITATIVE RESEARCH

While we have concentrated on polls (which is natural, given their central and historically important position in political marketing), we should be conscious of the substantial increase in popularity of focus groups and depth interviews as political marketing research tools. These two qualitative research methodologies are both quite regularly employed as a means of enabling political candidates and the news media to secure a better understanding of the appeal of politicians and election strategies, as well a host of "softer" and "broader" issues that are best understood in the light of the "probing nature" of qualitative research methods.

It is the "fabric" of qualitative research that so dramatically sets it apart from polling research. By its very nature, qualitative research methodologies tend to stress securing an understanding of underlying motivations or behavioral triggers (i.e., the "what-and-why," especially, the "why"). They also feature "what is being said"–that is what voters are saying, rather than what politicians may want to hear. In this capacity, qualitative research taps a different "strain" or dimension of individual voter's responses to a poll.

During the 2000 U.S. election period, a kind of *public forum focus group* emerged as a dramatic way of capturing and presenting a cross-section of voters' views on the issues and candidates. Sometimes, these public forum focus groups are presented by the news media in a series of short "video verbatim" of voters or citizens expressed viewpoints. In other cases, the news media dedicate larger blocks of time (from 20 to 45 minutes) to show the full sessions with respect to a particular issue. The news media's use of this form of focus group research seems to be a cross between a presentation of political research and an attempt to entertain their audiences with the diversity of the public's views on the issues.

Focus groups have not only proven valuable in allowing politicians to obtain a "picture" of the target voters' views, but they have also enabled them to learn what words or language the voters use to express their sentiment. Focus groups have also been quite useful in identifying the perceived strengths and weaknesses of particular candidates; gauging potential voters' perceptions of specific elements of a campaign strategy; or evaluating the visual and copy components of an advertising message.

THE INTERNET
AS A POLITICAL RESEARCH OPPORTUNITY

The appearance of news and political polling Web sites, as well as focus group or depth interview Web sites, are starting to provide some serious options to telephone polling, and other traditional forms of political marketing research. The Internet offers a relatively new opportunity for citizens to express their political views and for politicians and the news media to secure a "quick read" of the public's views on the issues.

In addition to Web-only political research sites, the more traditional broadcast and print news media have all embraced the Internet during the 2000 U.S. election as a means of securing and presenting viewers' opinions on the key political issues. The traditional news media, naturally see the Internet as a significant opportunity to secure more news content for their traditional audiences, as well as a new opportunity for the many individuals who visit their Web sites to secure the results of political polls, or some other form of political information.

Moreover, the increasingly high refusal rates experienced in telephone polling is likely placing increased pressure on the news media to develop more effective online polling methodologies. Just as telephone polls have replaced door-to-door polls; in the future we might expect that online polling will become a feasible alternative to telephone polling. Advocates of online polling point out that the Internet is a particularly convenient way of securing voters opinions. They suggest that research findings secured via the Internet are retrieved quickly and are more cost effective. In contrast, detractors warn that the exclusion of those demographic segments who do not have access to the Internet has the potential of producing inaccurate and misleading findings. Clearly, attention to providing improved online research methodologies and the opportunity for greater access to the Internet are priorities for those wanting to see Internet research grow.

WHAT DOES THE PUBLIC WANT FROM POLITICAL POLLS?

Potential voters are interested in securing a variety of information and guidance from polls and other forms of political marketing research. They are interested in contrasting their own views on the issues with those of other voters. Most important, voters are interested in determining whether their own views are being reflected in what politicians are saying. Also, hearing others views on the key issues is important to voters. Such insights have the power of confirming or strengthening voters' views, or sometimes they can cause voters' to rethink their views and possibly to see the virtue of a better option.

OUR RESEARCH

To explore consumers' perception and attitudes about polls, we recruited and trained college students from both a private suburban and a large public university in the New York metropolitan area to distribute a questionnaire on political marketing. The student recruiters were themselves precluded from participating in the survey.

The survey was undertaken several months after the 2000 U.S. presidential election. Each recruiter was responsible for six questionnaires (i.e., two questionnaires were to be completed by respondents who were 18-30 years of age, two questionnaires were to be completed by respondents who were 31-50 years of age, and two questionnaires were to be completed by respondents who were over 50). There was to be a "good mix" of males and females. At the end of this process we had 503 completed and usable questionnaires. Table 1 presents a profile of the respondents. It reveals that the respondents are:

- mostly Caucasian (54 percent)
- equally male and female
- mostly single (54 percent)
- well-educated (43 percent were at least college graduates)
- employed full-time (58 percent)
- dispersed across the full age and income spectrum

When it comes to political party affiliation, one half of the respondents were Democrats and one quarter were Republicans. The following section presents and discusses our findings.

RESULTS

In keeping with our second objective–to gauge our sample of voting age individuals' perceptions and attitudes related to political polls and polling–we asked our respondents reaction to (in terms of the extent to which they "agree" or "disagree") each of the following statements:

Political polls are very important for the average voter. [Q49]
Overall, political polls are a positive and have a positive influence. [Q55]
Political polls should not be given as much attention by the press and mass media. [Q50]
Political polls are important for the politicians, not for the voters. [Q52]
Political polls greatly influence the way people vote. [Q51]
I feel that political polls strongly influenced the way I voted in the 2000 Presidential election. [Q54]
I like political polls, because they give me something to talk about with others. [Q53]

TABLE 1. Profile of the Entire Sample (n = 503)

	Percent
Gender:	
Male	50
Female	50
Marital Status:	
Married	46
Single	54
Age:	
18-29	37
30-49	26
Over 50	37
Education Status:	
High School	21
Some College	36
College Graduate	28
Graduate Studies	15
Employment Status:	
Full-time	58
Part-time	19
Homemaker	5
Retired	11
Disabled	2
Unemployed	5
Income:	
Under $20,000	20
$20,000-$39,999	26
$40,000-$59,999	18
$60,000-$99,999	23
$100,000 or more	13
Race:	
White	54
African-American	13
Hispanic	14
Other	19
Political Affiliation:	
Republican	24
Democrat	49
Independent	13
None	14

What we found were somewhat complex attitudes about political polls.

In particular, our findings reveal that a substantial portion of the sample (i.e., about two-thirds) feel that political polls are very important for the average voter (see Figure 1), and that political polls greatly influence the way people vote (70 percent according to Figure 2). In contrast, to this vision that polls are an effective political strategic tool (i.e., it is both important and influential in its impact on voters), more than 65 percent of those surveyed feel that political polls do *not* generally have a positive influence or outcome (see Figure 3), and that they should *not* be given as much attention the press and mass media (Figure 4). Adding to this apparently paradoxical view (between Figure 1 and Figures 3 and

FIGURE 1. Political Polls Are Very Important for the Average Voter

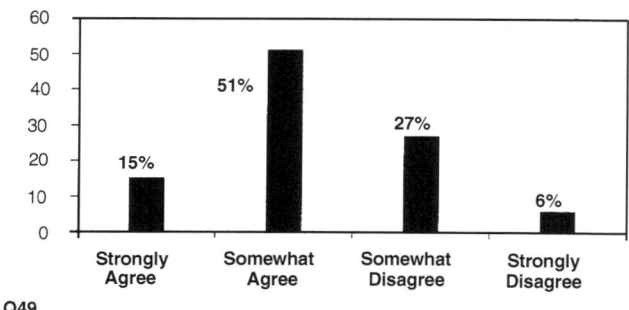

FIGURE 2. Political Polls Greatly Influence the Way People Vote

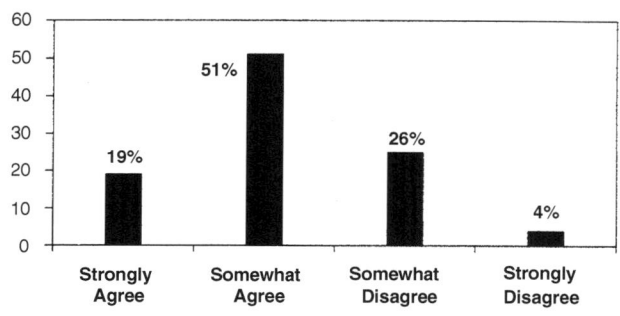

FIGURE 3. Overall, Political Polls Are Positive, and Have a Positive Influence

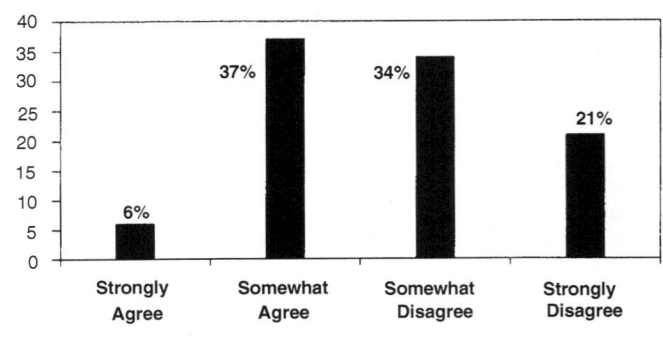

Q55

FIGURE 4. Political Polls Should Not Be Given as Much Attention

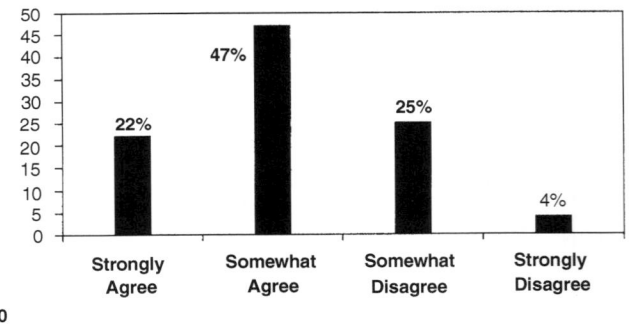

Q50

4), Figure 5 shows that more than 60 percent of our respondents feel that political polls are important for politicians, not for voters.

What seems to shed some light on this complex impression of polling is the finding in Figure 6 which show that only 25 percent of our respondents feel that political polls strongly influenced the way *that they* [our emphasis] voted in the 2000 Presidential election. In other words, our respondents draw a major distinction between "themselves" and their fellow voters–that is, the polls influences "others," but *not* "me" (see Figure 7). However, a related question, with respect to "liking" political polls because they give me something to talk about with others, reveals

FIGURE 5. Political Polls Are Important for the Politicians, Not for the Voters

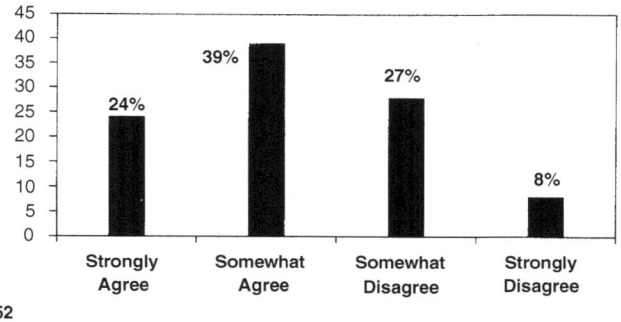

Q52

FIGURE 6. I Feel That Political Polls Strongly Influenced the Way I Voted in the 2000 Presidential Election

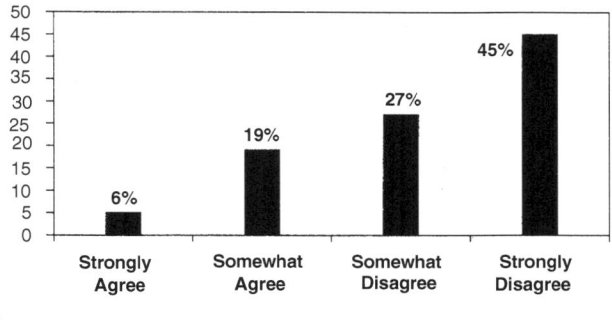

Q54

that 38 percent of our respondents agree with this statement (see Figure 8). So for the respondents (i.e., the "me" in contrast to the "others"), polls are not perceived to be particularly influential when it comes to how they might vote; yet polls are nevertheless appreciated by almost 40 percent of the respondents when it comes to providing them a basis for political discussions with others.

CONCLUSIONS

This article first explored the landscape of the use of political marketing research, with particular attention given to polling. As our discus-

FIGURE 7. Comparison of "Them and Me" in Terms of the Influence of Polls on Voting

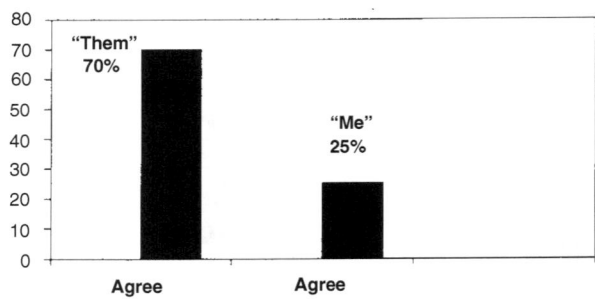

FIGURE 8. I Like Political Polls, Because They Give Me Something to Talk About with Others

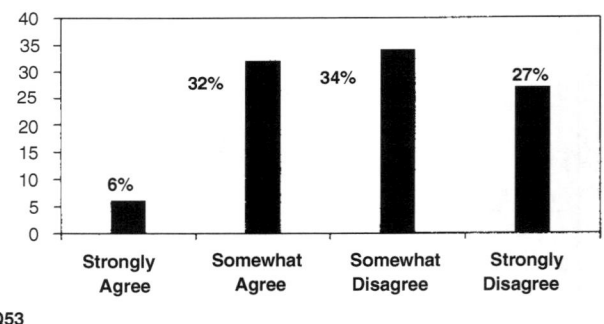

Q53

sion indicates, the role of pollsters is changing. They are becoming, in many instances, key political strategists. The best-known pollsters appear on the news media to share their insights; and some use their Web sites to present selections from their research findings, or provide a forum on political issues. However, one of the most important responsibilities of pollsters, and for that matter the news media, seems to be to inform the public as to how to decide whether a poll's results are valid and reliable. The public often does not know much about sampling procedures, or even what "confidence levels" or "margins of error" mean.

An appreciation of the basics of polling can aid voters in evaluating the veracity of the data obtained from a particular poll. Poorly worded or improperly worded questions can skew results. As political marketing research and polling grows in popularity, pollsters and other political researchers have a professional obligation to provide unbiased results.

The second objective of this research was to examine some exploratory research on voting-age respondents' views on polls and their impact. The complex and "colliding findings" seem to suggest a dichotomy between how the respondents see polls impacting "others," and how they see polls influencing their own views and actions. Specifically, the findings indicate that while respondents tend to feel that polls are important and influential when it comes to the way others will vote, they tend to feel that when it comes to themselves that political polls are not influential. However, nearly 40 percent feel that polls provide them with things to discuss with others. Ultimately, these findings about polls, appear to reveal a "me" versus "others" vision of the impact of polls. In seeking some other insights that might shed light on these findings, we identified research that suggests that 50 percent of regular CNN viewers are very interested in political polls, and 45 percent believe that polls give you a better understanding of the news (Gallup, 1999). However, 51 percent of their viewers report that polls "do not help," and 67 percent indicate that the media pays too much attention to polls. Again, suggesting a complex and out-of-sync view of political polling. Still further, 54 percent of the CNN respondents said politicians pay too much attention to polls.

Like own research, the CNN research suggests that "consumers of polls" appear to be quite fickle in their views of political marketing research. Ultimately, we need to further explore this dynamic and complex picture of political polls in order to better understand the underlying dynamic of people's attitudes and actions.

REFERENCES

Babad, Elisha and Eitan Yacabos, "Wish and Reality in Voters' Predictions of Election Outcomes," *Political Psychology*, 14, March 1993, 37-42.

Benedetto, Richard and Drinkard, Jim, "As Political Polls Grow, So Does Their Influence," *USA Today*, September 13, 2000, A1.

Borger, Julian, "TV Giants Admit Poll Shambles," *The Guardian*, February 15, 2001, 17.

Buell, John, "Media Myopia and the Future of Democratic Politics," *The Humanist*, Jan/Feb 2001, 61, 1, 35-36.

Chin, Mangyee, "Undecided Voters: Do Political Polls Cast Their Vote?" Unpublished Master's Paper, (Hempstead, NY: Hofstra University September, 2001).

Harwood, John and Cynthia Crossen, "Head Counting: Why Many New Polls Put Different Spins on Presidential Contest and Plunge in Public Response Rates Tax an Inexact Science," *Wall Street Journal*, September 29, 2000, A1.

Jacobs, Lawrence R. and Robert Y. Shapiro, "Presidential Manipulation of Polls and Public Opinion: The Nixon Administration and the Pollster," *Political Science Quarterly*, Winter 1995-1996, 223-245.

Katz, John, "Hail the Polls: The Public's Word, Edgewise," *Freedom Forum*, 2001, (www.freedomforum.org).

Morwitz, Vicki G. and Carol Pluzinski, "Do Polls Reflect Opinions or Do Opinions Reflect Polls? The Impact of Political Polling on Voter's Expectations, Preferences, and Behavior," *Journal of Consumer Research*, 23, June 1996, 53-67.

Newman, Bruce, *The Marketing of the President* (Thousand Oaks, CA: Sage Publications, 1994).

Pobst, Kevin, "Understanding Political Polls: A Key Citizenship Skill for the 21st Century," *Social Education*, November/December 1999, 401-418.

Steinhorn, Leonard and Carroll, Maurice, "Symposium: Q Does the Reliance of the News Media on Polls Distort Polling?" *Insight on the News*, December 25, 2000, 2-7.

Teachout, Terry, "Republican Nation, Democratic Nation?" *Commentary*, 3, January 2001, 23-29.

The 2000 American Presidential Election: Lessons from the Closest Contest in American History

Dennis W. Johnson

The George Washington University, USA

SUMMARY. The 2000 Presidential election was one of the longest, most expensive and closest in American history. It was the Presidential election that exposed the flaws (or genius) of the electoral college system, demonstrated the imperfections of media dependency on exit polls and quick election calling, and showed how a third party candidate with just two percent of the popular vote could make the difference in the crucial state of Florida. Democrats lost states they should have won; Republicans lost every big city and most of their suburbs; and the Florida election came down to a five-to-four muddled decision by the Supreme Court. Americans collectively learned a great civics lesson: that even in a bitter, controversial contest, our candidates accept defeat graciously; the

Dennis W. Johnson is Associate Dean at the Graduate School of Political Management, The George Washington University, Washington, DC (E-mail: dwjgspm@gwu.edu). He is author of *No Place for Amateurs: How Political Consultants Are Reshaping American Democracy* (Routledge, 2001) and is currently Principal Investigator for the Congress Online Project, a joint research project of The George Washington University and the Congressional Management Foundation, funded by the Pew Charitable Trusts. Dr. Johnson's current research interests include international political consulting and electronic advocacy and governance.

[Haworth co-indexing entry note]: "The 2000 American Presidential Election: Lessons from the Closest Contest in American History." Johnson, Dennis W. Co-published simultaneously in *Journal of Political Marketing* (The Haworth Political Press, an imprint of The Haworth Press, Inc.) Vol. 1, No. 2/3, 2002, pp. 69-87; and: *Communication of Politics: Cross-Cultural Theory Building in the Practice of Public Relations and Political Marketing* (eds: Bruce I. Newman, and Dejan Verčič) The Haworth Political Press, an imprint of The Haworth Press, Inc., 2002, pp. 69-87. Single or multiple copies of this article are available for a fee from The Haworth Document Delivery Service [1-800-HAWORTH, 9:00 a.m. - 5:00 p.m. (EST). E-mail address: getinfo@haworthpressinc.com].

10.1300/J199v01n02_06

simple act of voting is not so simple; and that for all its shortcomings, the electoral college did work. *[Article copies available for a fee from The Haworth Document Delivery Service: 1-800-HAWORTH. E-mail address: <getinfo@haworthpressinc.com> Website: <http://www.HaworthPress.com> © 2002 by The Haworth Press, Inc. All rights reserved.]*

KEYWORDS. 2000 Presidential election, Al Gore, George W. Bush, Florida, Electoral College, exit polls, political consultants, American political campaigns, Ralph Nader, U.S. Supreme Court, election law

The 2000 Presidential election was the closest American Presidential election in history. In the popular vote, Vice President Albert Gore, Jr., bested Texas Governor George W. Bush by 550,000 votes out of a total of 101,452,000 cast between them; and in the deciding electoral vote, Bush beat Gore by 4 votes, winning one more than the minimum needed to be declared the winner outright. It was also one of the longest and was the most expensive contests. This was a campaign filled with interesting twists and turns, but with the most excitement and suspense coming after the contest was over.

It was one of the longest Presidential contests because two years before the election, Republican party leaders were lining up behind George W. Bush as the best chance to take back the White House. Republican leaders were chagrined when old party faithful Bob Dole captured the party's nomination in 1996, only to find him a very weak opponent in the general election against incumbent President Bill Clinton. Republican leaders were determined that for the 2000 race, the strongest candidate would be placed in nomination. Democrats, too, were lining up quickly behind Vice President Al Gore as the best hope for retaining the White House after the tumultuous Clinton years. The frontrunners, however, were challenged, especially by a vigorous fight for the Republican Party primary nomination by Arizona Senator John McCain, and a more lack-luster challenge in the Democratic Party by former New Jersey Senator Bill Bradley.

The 2000 election was by all measure the most expensive campaign in history. Altogether the presidential candidate of both parties raised $528 million, compared to $425 million in 1996. George W. Bush raised $191 million, including federal funds, while Al Gore raised $133 million. Bush outraised Gore in every state but three and the District of

Columbia (Center for Responsive Politics, 2001). When political party money is added, along with unregulated issue advocacy funds, it is estimated that the cost of the 2000 presidential election easily topped a billion dollars.

Senator John McCain made headlines for his fund-raising capabilities over the Internet. At one point during the primaries, when his campaign was on fire, McCain managed to raise a million dollars from online sources in just one day. The Internet, eagerly anticipated (but yet to live up to the hype) as the new magic campaign tool, has provided a new way to tap into voters' pockets. Steve Forbes continued throwing away the family fortune in another self-deluding run for the Republican nomination.

In a stroke of good fortune for both nominees, their choices for Vice President, former White House insider and Secretary of Defense Richard Cheney for the Republicans and Senator Joseph Lieberman of Connecticut for the Democrats, added significantly to the tickets. This was far different from George Bush (senior) in 1988 choosing the untested and unprepared Senator Dan Quayle, or Bob Dole selecting former Housing Secretary Jack Kemp in 1996, neither of whom added to their respective Republican tickets.

We knew that the contest between Gore and Bush would be very close, because Americans were reminded almost daily with a new poll revealing the thin margins. In 2000, public polling was omnipresent: all day, every day, by more and more polling organizations. At any one time, between 25 and 40 polls were being taken by research firms, the media, universities and others, starting in early summer. There was also a great number of online surveys conducted. The great majority of these polls, however, were methodologically flawed, and came in for heavy criticism by professional polling organizations. Nonetheless, many of those polls were reported by the media, often without any warning that they were fundamentally flawed and unreliable.

Republicans and Democrats continued the trend seen in their 1996 national conventions–noncontroversial theater and made-for-television events. However, solid and exceptional speeches were given by both Bush and Gore. Relatively few Americans watched the conventions on television, specially-developed Internet sites found a disappointingly small audience, and the image that stuck in most people's minds was Al Gore's impassioned, lengthy kiss of his wife Tipper after his acceptance speech.

The election, though a dead heat for the last four months, was surprisingly calm. There were no great blunders, no dramatic flourishes, no revelations of misdeeds, no great oratory, and no grand schemes promised. George W. Bush, though somewhat unsteady during the debates, proved that he could stand up to the seasoned and prepared Vice President. On election night, attention turned to Florida, but this election went well beyond Florida and well beyond election night.

THE RESULTS

In this most unusual contest, George W. Bush won the Electoral College with one vote to spare. He needed 270 of the 538 electoral votes to win; he received 271. Not since the Thomas Jefferson-Aaron Burr electoral deadlock of 1800 had any candidate ever won with such a small margin in the Electoral College. Al Gore won the total popular vote by 550,000. Not since 1888 had a losing presidential candidate won the popular vote but lost the Electoral College vote. Table 1 gives the results of the 2000 Presidential election.

THE GREAT DIVIDE

The 2000 electoral map is a study in marked contrasts. As Table 2 indicates, except for New Hampshire, Al Gore won the populous Northeast and mid-Atlantic area; George W. Bush won all of the South, all of the Great Plains, and all of the Rocky Mountain states, except New Mexico. Gore won all of the Pacific coast states, except for Alaska. Only the Midwest was truly competitive. How different from years past, when the South was solidly Democratic, where New England was reliably Republican, and where the Midwest was a bastion of Republican strength.

TABLE 1. 2000 National Presidential Summary

Candidate	Electoral Vote	Popular Vote	Percentage
George W. Bush (R)	271	50,456,169	48.101
Al Gore (D)	267	50,996,116	48.383
Ralph Nader (Green)	0	2,831,066	2.710

TABLE 2. Electoral College Vote by Region

Region	States for Bush	States for Gore
New England	New Hampshire (4)	Maine, Vermont, Massachusetts, Connecticut, Rhode Island (total: 27)
Mid-Atlantic	West Virginia (5)	New York, Pennsylvania, New Jersey, Delaware, Maryland, District of Columbia (total: 87)
South	Virginia, North Carolina, South Carolina, Georgia, Kentucky, Tennessee, Alabama, Mississippi, Florida, Louisiana, Arkansas (total: 123)	
Midwest	Ohio, Indiana, Missouri (total: 44)	Michigan, Wisconsin, Illinois, Minnesota, Iowa (total: 68)
Great Plains and Rockies	North Dakota, South Dakota, Nebraska, Kansas, Oklahoma, Texas, Colorado, Wyoming, Montana, Idaho, Utah, Arizona, Nevada (total: 92)	New Mexico: 5
Pacific	Alaska: 3	California, Oregon, Washington, Hawaii (total: 76)

An analysis of the vote in individual counties demonstrates another dimension of this great divide. Gore was the winner in virtually every big city *and many of their suburbs*, while Bush won nearly all of small town and rural America. Gore won only 676 counties (less than half of what Clinton won in 1996), while Bush won an incredible 2,477 counties.

There were other divides as well:

- Whites favored Bush (54 to 42 percent)
- Blacks favored Gore (90 to 9 percent)
- Married voters favored Bush (53 to 44 percent)
- Single voters favored Gore (57 to 38 percent)
- Those making less than $30,000 per year favored Gore (54 to 41 percent)
- Those making more than $100,000 per year favored Bush (54 to 43 percent)

Not in just Florida, but in other states as well, the margins of victory were razor-thin. There was less than one percentage point difference between Gore and Bush in Oregon, Iowa, and New Mexico. States thought highly probable for Bush, like Florida, Pennsylvania or Michigan, became highly vulnerable; for Gore, his home state of Tennessee, West Virginia, Arkansas, and New Hampshire should have been securely his, but he lost all four.

With tracking polls running constantly since mid-summer, with nearly all of them showing a dead heat, the contest became one of play-it-safe strategy, political triage, nail-biting, and ultimately, raw political brokering.

THE CONSULTANTS

Senior political consultants working for presidential candidates have often had a rocky time. The 1988 team working for Democrat Michael Dukakis had a difficult time countering attacks against them by the more nimble, aggressive, and politically adept Republican consulting team led by Lee Atwater. The 1992 team of Republican consultants for the Bush-Quayle re-election never could reach its stride, failing in the most elemental way to convince voters why George Bush should be re-elected. The 1996 Republican team for Bob Dole and Jack Kemp was a revolving door of consultants, characterized as "one of the most hapless campaigns in modern political history" (Thomas, 1997; Johnson, 2001). In the meantime, Clinton consultants James Carville (in 1992) and Dick Morris (in 1996) became household names, while more anonymous, but effective consultants like Stanley Greenberg and Mandy Grunwald (1992), Robert Squier and Mark Penn (1996) worked on strategy, media and message.

The Republican and Democratic consulting teams in 2000 both had their hands full. The Bush team (Karl Rove, Karen Hughes, Joe Allbaugh) had to defend their candidate's position as front runner, to stave-off the charge of primary opponent Senator John McCain, and go into the general election with plenty of cash on-hand (and plenty of money already spent), as the underdog against a sitting Vice President. The Democratic consulting team (Tony Coehlo–later replaced by William Daley, Carter Eskew, Donna Brazille) had its own challenges. By most calculations, this was Gore's election to lose. With the economy strong, Gore should have had a decisive edge; with a string of accomplishments during his term as Vice President, he should have been able to convince voters that he was ready to lead the nation. But the Gore team lost footing and valuable time. In an attempt to quash vicious in-fighting and second-guessing, Gore abruptly moved his campaign headquarters from Washington to Nashville. Gore was uncomfortable finding the right message and image, even the right clothes to wear; and more importantly, determining just where President Clinton, faults and all, would fit into the Gore election campaign.

As the race turned out, neither set of consultants made fatal mistakes, and as the campaign tightened, neither side would risk departing from their own game plans, which were driven by internal tracking polls. The 2000 race brought an entirely unexpected set of consultants to prominence, election law specialists and constitutional lawyers. Playing a significant role for Al Gore was his former chief of staff, Ron Klain, who was unceremoniously dropped from the election team early in the campaign, but made a critical reappearance after the election to fight the recount battle in the courts.

THE FLAWED EXIT POLLS IN FLORIDA

Exit polls have become important tools for election day media reporting. Developed under the pioneering work of Warren Mitofsky, exit polls give journalists and candidates an early view on election day of voting patterns and trends, forecasting hours ahead of the closing time of how the final vote will end up. To make exit polls accurate predictors of actual outcomes, the precincts used for the exit interviews, the voter demographics, and past voting history must all be chosen with great care (Lavrakas & Holley, 1991).

What happened in Florida turned out to be a news maker's nightmare, what *Washington Post* media critic Howard Kurtz called the "biggest blunder in television history on election night" (Kurtz, 2000). As election night grew longer and more tense, it became evident that whoever won Florida would become the president. This put added pressure on the network television stations to be accurate, but also to be first in reporting. The anxious networks–CBS, NBC, ABC, CNN, and Fox News–each declared Al Gore as the winner, then retracted Gore's win and announced that George Bush had won; later they retracted Bush's victory, and finally they all had publicly to admit that the race was too close to call.

The networks all came to the same erroneous conclusions because they were all relying on one source for their predictive information, the exit poll data provided by Voter News Services (VNS). In 1993, the networks, in a cost cutting move, decided to pool their resources and created VNS to be their one source for exit poll data. No one had anticipated that the data and the conclusions drawn from VNS exit polls would be fatally flawed and have such major consequences.

In an internal VNS report released weeks after the election, several major problems had been found with the data. First, VNS had greatly underestimated the size of the absentee vote: the assumed vote was 7.2 percent, while the actual absentee vote was 12 percent. Second, VNS predicted 22.4 percent of the absentee vote would go to Bush, while the actual numbers were 23.7 percent. Third, the 2000 exit poll results were being compared to 1998 Florida gubernatorial election rather than the 1996 Florida presidential election. The rationale was that because Florida is such a fast-growing state, it would be better to compare with the most recent election, 1998. But the 1996 election results still would have produced a better comparative sample: presidential contests are different from gubernatorial contests, in that they bring out more citizens to vote, especially more independents. Relying on the 1998 voting data skewed the 2000 exit polls predictions in favor of Gore. Fourth, there was evidence that the 2000 exit polls overestimated African American voters (heavily Democratic), while underestimating Cuban-American voters (strongly Republican).

The Florida vote was so close, with Bush winning by less than 600 votes (and the precise count is still unknown) out of over 6 million votes cast. No matter how finely tuned the exit polls could be, they could never have predicted the winner with any degree of certitude. The only right exit poll answer on election night was that Florida was "too close to call." Nevertheless, the damage had been done. The credibility of both the media and the polling industry suffered from the miscalculations of VNS and the eagerness of the media to report faulty numbers. The six members of the Voter News Service–ABC, NBC, CBS, CNN, Fox News and the Associated Press–announced on June 1, 2001 that they would retain VNS and revamp its operations. The likely changes include updating computer systems, improving statistical models and coming up with a better way for assessing absentee ballots (AP, 2001).

FLORIDA BALLOTING AND RECOUNTS

For many months early in the campaign, it was assumed by the candidates and political strategists that Florida would easily go Republican. It was the home of Governor Jeb Bush, brother of the Republican nominee, the state has increasingly become conservative and Republican in presidential years, and the important Cuban-American population was seething over the Clinton Administration's handling of the Elian Gonzales episode. The supposedly safe Republican state became a toss up when Joseph Lieberman was chosen as the Democratic Vice Presidential candidate. Lieberman of Connecticut, the first Jewish candidate for nationwide office, immediately attracted the critical bloc of Jewish voters in South Florida. Suddenly, Florida was a hotly-contested, critical state in cobbling together an Electoral College majority.

Nothing had prepared the U.S. public or Florida election officials for the aftermath of the razor-thin margins found on election day (see Table 3). The day following the elections, a provision of Florida law went into effect that required an automatic recount in each of the 67 counties.

The Florida recount put the harsh spotlight on the most basic of democratic acts. What followed was, in the assessment of political reporters John Mintz and Peter Slevin, "a confounding array of vague laws, arbitrary local decisions and erratic leadership by Florida Secretary of State Katherine Harris's office" (Mintz & Slevin, 2001). While it was the specific and first duty of the Florida Secretary of State to "maintain uniformity" in the state's elections, the counties, notoriously independent, used broad discretion in determining which votes counted and which were to be recounted.

Florida state election law required an automatic recount because of the closeness of the election. But 18 of the state's 67 counties never recounted; they simply checked their original results. Altogether, 1.58 million votes (out of over 6 million cast) had not been counted a second

TABLE 3. Results of Florida Presidential Balloting

Candidate, Party	Votes	Percentage
George W. Bush, Republican	2,912,790	49
Al Gore, Democrat	2,912,253	49
Ralph Nader, Green	97,488	2
Pat Buchanan, Reform	17,484	0
Harry Browne, Libertarian	16,415	0
John Hagelin, Natural Law	2,281	0
Monica Moorehead, Workers of the World	1,804	0
Howard Phillips, Constitutional	1,322	0
David McReynolds, Socialist	622	0
James Harris, Socialist Workers	562	0

time, as required by state law. Much of the attention focused on faulty or antiquated voting machines, giving Americans a new vocabulary of "hanging chads" and "pregnant chads." But optical scanning machines had their troubles as well. Thousands of ballots were left uncounted when submitted to an optical scan because voters had circled or put a check mark by their candidate instead of blackening in the box. Other ballots were disqualified because voters used their own pens with the wrong color ink. Some counties had machines that rejected ballots that were wrongly marked, and the voters were given a second chance to vote. But other counties with optical scans did not have the equipment to detect errors; and some counties with the error-detecting equipment chose not to use it. Mintz and Slevin conclude that as many as 120,000 Florida ballots could have been corrected by voters if every county had used modern machines with second-chance technology.

In an attempt to weed out "probable" felons, the state elections division sent to the counties the names of thousands of persons who were not felons, but, nevertheless, were to be purged from the voting rolls. Some counties used the faulty list, others ignored it. The state did nothing to reconcile the differences. In Osceola County, with a Hispanic population of 29 percent, the county elections supervisor refused to print the ballot in Spanish, even though federal law requires two languages in counties where at least 5 percent of the population has deficiencies in English. Democratic officials complained that many Hispanics were confused and could not tell the difference between "Libertarian" (the party of Harry Browne), and "Lieberman" (the Democratic Vice Presidential candidate whose name appeared just below the word "Libertarian"). The notorious "butterfly" ballot, innocently designed in large type to help elderly voters, confused many people. An independent analysis by the *Washington Post* estimated that Gore lost about 6,500 votes as a result of voter error or confusion over the butterfly ballot: citizens who thought they were voting for Gore-Lieberman were actually voting for Reform candidate Patrick Buchanan. Also a disproportionate number of people using the butterfly ballot mistakenly voted for two candidates, one from each column, and as a consequence had their ballots disqualified.

Roughly 9,000 undervotes were found in Dade County and had not been recounted, with many of the voting irregularities occurring in African-American communities, which had overwhelmingly supported Gore. It was discovered that African-American ballots were far more likely to be spoiled and deemed invalid than other ballots. This only added to the undercurrent of distrust among African-Americans in Florida and the Democratic Party.

A number of citizens were told that they were not registered to vote, when in fact they knew that they had registered when they obtained or renewed their driver's license. Since 1995, the state motor vehicle agency had processed 570,000 new voter registration forms, along with new or renewed vehicle registrations. But computer glitches abounded in the voter registration software; motor vehicle employees sometimes failed to complete the voter registration forms, and required signatures were missing, and motor vehicle agencies simply failed to deliver the registration forms to the county election boards on time.

THE BATTLE IN THE COURTS

For the first time in history, the Supreme Court of the United States had a direct and immediate impact on the election of the President. Its 5 to 4 decision, along party and ideological lines, on December 12, halted any further recount of ballots, stopping the Gore uphill battle to gain precious votes, and effectively handed the Presidency over to George W. Bush.

The torturous path to the December 12th decision began with the Florida Secretary of State Katherine Harris, a Republican insider whose every key interpretation of Florida law benefitted the Bush campaign. Aiding her was one of Florida's most experienced and toughest political strategists, J. M. "Mac" Stipanovich (Von Drehle et al., 2001). One of the key decisions was to strictly enforce the state required that election results be certified within seven days (November 13), and not permit an extension. Unexpectedly, the Florida State Supreme Court ordered Harris not to certify the election and further ordered recounts to continue. That decision was rebuffed by the U.S. Supreme Court, which required further clarity in its intent. There were many sideshows: county and city officials making their own decisions as to what to recount, apply their own standards, some eager to recount, many not, and some used a variety of delaying tactics. The Republican-dominated state legislature threatened to seize the decision from the courts and make up its own mind as to the validity of the elections. Multiple lawsuits in both federal and state courts were filed by individuals and organizations, in addition to the principal cases, the Florida Supreme Court decision and then the U.S. Supreme Court case. Finally, the Florida Supreme Court on December 8, by a 4 to 3 vote issued a broad decision: all undervotes, not just those requested in Miami-Dade County, were to be reexamined.

Both the Republican and Democratic campaign teams sent their public relations emissaries (headed by grey eminences Warren Christopher for the Democrats and James A. Baker III for the Republicans), and their election and constitutional law experts (Ron Klain, Walter Dellinger, Lawrence Tribe, and especially David Boies for the Democrats, and George J. Terwilliger III, Benjamin Ginsberg, and Theodore Olson for the Republicans).

The day following the Florida Supreme Court's sweeping decision, the U.S. Supreme Court ordered an immediate halt to the recount effort. Then after listening to arguments by both parties in *Gore v. Bush*, the Supreme Court on December 12 handed down its final word. By a 5 to 4 vote, right down ideological lines, the Court in an "unlovely and hastily composed pile of opinions, dissents, half-agreements and bitter recriminations" ruled that all recounting must cease (Von Drehle et al., 2001a). Soon thereafter, Vice President Gore conceded defeat.

That democratic truism, "every vote counts," had been turned into a Gore campaign war cry over Florida votes: "count every vote." This election gave both phrases new meaning: Bush had won Florida by less than one-hundredth of one percent, and thus carried the Electoral College by one vote; made possible by a U. S. Supreme Court majority of one.

LOSING TENNESSEE AND WEST VIRGINIA

The Gore loss in Florida was not the only factor. No major presidential candidate should ever lose his home state. Even Walter Mondale, who was shellacked by Ronald Reagan in 1984, managed (barely) to win his home state of Minnesota, plus the District of Columbia. He won no other state, but at least Mondale held onto his political power base. Al Gore had the dubious distinction of losing his home state of Tennessee, with 47 percent of the vote for Gore and 51 percent for Bush. The Gore family has deep roots in Tennessee political history, with the patriarch, Al Gore, Sr. having served as U.S. Senator and as contender for the vice presidential nomination of the Democratic Party. Al Gore, Jr., had been groomed for politics, serving eight years as Congressman, eight years as U.S. Senator, then eight years as Vice President of the United States. While he may have kept good ties to his district and state during his legislative years, he had apparently lost that connection with Tennessee during his years as Vice President. In the meantime, Tennessee was becoming more conservative and like many other Southern states, becoming much more of a Republican stronghold.

Gore also lost one of the most Democratic states in the union, West Virginia. Democratic strategists could always rely on this small, relatively poor state, with its dependency on the federal government, to cast its five electoral votes in the Democratic column. But in 2000, Bush received 52 percent of the West Virginia vote while Gore received just 46 percent of the vote.

An important factor that accounted for the loss of these two states (plus Arkansas, Missouri, and Louisiana), was the concerted, strategic efforts of the National Rifle Association to activate support from its members and get them out to vote for Bush. Gun owners strongly supported Bush, 61 percent to 36 percent for Gore. Always a potent force, the gun lobby exerted its grassroots muscle for Bush in these decisive states.

From a political strategist's point of view, any candidate who cannot win his home state and cannot win one of his party's most reliable states, doesn't deserve to be president.

RALPH NADER

Another reason Al Gore is not president is the impact of reformist gadfly Ralph Nader on the presidential ballot. Nader had run for president in 1996, with hardly anyone noticing him on the ballot. He was nearly invisible that year because President Bill Clinton handily defeated Republican challenger Bob Dole, and third party candidates, including Nader, were merely historical footnotes. This time around, however, Ralph Nader and the Green Party made history: in the one state that counted the most, Florida, the 97,488 votes garnered by Nader tipped the balance. Had just 600 of those votes gone for Gore, George W. Bush would have been deprived of the presidency. In the intense media interest surrounding ballot recounts and "hanging chads," the Nader factor has all but been lost. But it certainly was not lost on Democratic activists who still seethe when the name of Ralph Nader is mentioned.

Nader was the candidate of the Green Party, a "ragamuffin collection of anti-globalists, campaign finance aficionados, and health care and labor activists" and disaffected liberals (Powell, 2000). Nationwide Nader and his running mate, Winona LaDuke, an American Indian activist, gathered a mere 2.7 percent of the vote. Earlier third party candidates had done much better than Nader in overall percentage of their nationwide vote for President: businessman Ross Perot (Reform Party), running twice in the 1990s, Congressman John Anderson (Independent) running in 1980; Alabama governor George Wallace (American Independent Party), running twice in 1968 then 1972. Only Wallace, predominantly a southern regional candidate, actually carried any state.

Nader, in polls taken just weeks before the election, was showing support of 7-8 percent of the electorate. That was a solid number for a third party candidate, and one that would assure that the Green Party would meet the 5 percent threshold to receive federal matching dollars for its campaign in 2004. But on election night, apparently many disaffected liberal Democrats voted with their head (for Gore) and not with their heart (for Nader).

Nader and the Green Party also had some impact at the grassroots level. The Greens ran 238 candidates in 32 states, and had 20 of their candidates win, primarily in local contests in Western states. Green candidates gathered enough votes to deprive three Democrats from gaining congressional seats (Powell, 2000).

THE ELECTORAL COLLEGE

For well over 100 years, the Electoral College had worked smoothly in presidential elections. The last time that a presidential candidate, like George W. Bush, had received the majority of electoral votes but failed to get the majority of the popular vote was in 1888, when Benjamin Harrison won with narrow margins in 20 states, while incumbent President Grover Cleveland rang up huge majorities in 18 states. Like the 2000 contest, the difference between the popular vote was less than one percentage point.

The Electoral College, long considered by many as an antiquated eighteenth century artifact, is the fundamental constitutional mechanism governing our presidential elections. Each state is allocated a number of electors equal to the number of its two U.S. Senators plus the number of its U.S. Representatives. The political parties in each state submit to the chief election official of that state a list of individuals pledged to their candidate, in equal number to the number of electors assigned to the state. While voters may think they are casting ballots for candidates, they are technically choosing electors. The ballots on election day almost always contain in fine print the words "electors for" in front of each of the candidates. Whichever party slate wins the most popular votes in the state becomes that state's electors–winner take all (except in Maine and Nebraska where two electors are chosen by statewide popular vote and the remainder by the popular vote of each congressional district) (Kimberling, n.d.).

On the Monday following the second Wednesday of December, each state's electors meet in their respective state capitals and cast their vote. In every election, except 2000, this was a foregone conclusion, with the excitement and drama culminating on election day, and the meeting of electors six weeks later as nothing more than a formality.

Inevitably, the history of 1888 would repeat itself, and the winner of the Electoral College vote would not have the majority of the popular vote. Immediately following election night, there were cries for reforming or even abolishing the Electoral College. In one of her first statements as Senator-elect, Hillary Clinton announced that she would introduce legislation to abolish the Electoral College. However, the call for abolishing or reforming the Electoral College reform quickly died down. To make such a fundamental change would require a constitutional amendment, always difficult to accomplish, which would have to be passed by the states, many of which might lose the little leverage they have through the Electoral College mechanism. Such a change would also invite a nasty fight over minority rights and the two-party system. Instead of revamping the Electoral College, states are turning to the more pressing issue: updating ballot machines, upgrading voter registration software, and fixing the general mechanisms of voting.

IF ONLY, IF ONLY

Gnawing away at political strategist and Democratic loyalist for years to come will be those unsolvable questions–if only . . .

* The media didn't prematurely and erroneously flash "Bush Wins!" on election night and if Gore hadn't conceded defeat that evening. What the country was then left with was the impression that Bush had won, and that all the protestations by Gore afterwards were coming from the second-place finisher who was trying to take the election away from the victor.
* The state election offices and the state governorship of Florida were not under the control of ardent Republicans, Secretary of State Katherine Harris, and brother Jeb Bush.
* The Supreme Court of the United States decided not to intervene, the decision may have rested with the Supreme Court of Florida, which ruled for a more complete recount.
* Ralph Nader hadn't entered as a third party candidate.

- Gore had held onto his home state of Tennessee and its 11 electoral votes; he could have won the Presidency even while losing Florida. The same for West Virginia with its 5 electoral votes: had Gore won there, while losing Florida and Tennessee, he would have been elected President.

- Gore hadn't won the next three closest contests. Gore won in Iowa (7 electoral votes) by just 4,000 votes out of 1.6 million cast–or one-quarter of one percent. Gore won New Mexico (5 electoral votes) by 350 votes out of 560,000 cast–or 6 hundreds of one percent. Republican strategists point out that a freak snow storm hit New Mexico on election day, dumping snow (and depressing voter turnout) in Republican strongholds! Gore won Oregon (7 electoral votes) by 6,800 votes out of 1.4 million cast–less than one-half of one percent. These three states together, however, would still not have made the difference. Their combined 22 electoral votes did not add up to the much more important prize of Florida's 25 electoral votes.

Could the Gore campaign have developed a more productive targeting strategy? Could Gore not have slipped as badly if he didn't come across as aggressive and know-it-all in the debates? Could Gore have swallowed hard, tucked in his pride, and asked President Clinton to campaign for him in crucial swing states? Should Gore have emphasized, not downplayed, the real and substantial policy achievements of the Clinton-Gore years?

These and other scenarios could haunt Gore, Lieberman, and the Democratic political strategist for years to come, or it could energize them to prepare for a rough, vigorous fight in 2004. The pill of defeat has a bitter, long-lasting aftertaste.

CONCLUSION

This unprecedented presidential election had made election officials, legislators and citizens rethink some of the most basic aspects of campaigns and elections. The American presidential election, held out to many throughout the world as the shining example of democracy at work, came under intense scrutiny, pressure, and even ridicule. What had worked so well for so long seemed to break down. But, in fact, at its fundamental core, the democratic election system did not break down. The reality was that the election was just so close that any irregularities were magnified beyond proportion. But the close election also revealed fissures that were not exposed in early elections.

Thanks to the 2000 election, we learned several things:

The Simple Act of Voting is not so simple. The chaos and human error found in the Florida recount episode could have happened nearly anywhere in the United States. Software glitches, faulty voter registration lists, antiquated voting machines, failure to design ballots that are clearly understandable and unambiguous, failure to enforce laws requiring uniformity in ballot counting, discretion of local officials in using various balloting machines and in interpreting results–all of these could have happened virtually anywhere in the United States. The inadequacies of voting booth practices have only been masked by elections that have not had the harsh scrutiny of the Florida Presidential election or have not been as close in their outcome. Election officials throughout the United States, in reviewing the sad spectacle of Florida recounts, must have been murmuring, "There, but for the grace of God, go I."

A year later, an exhaustive study was conducted by several media organizations of 175,010 ballots cast in Florida but not counted by election officials. The conclusion was that George W. Bush would still have won the state and thus the presidency under two limited, but never completed, recounts. Yet, if there were a statewide recount, Al Gore would have won a narrow victory.

In response to the voting fiasco, the state of Florida eliminated the punch-card voting system (and its hanging chads), and allocated $24 million for new voting machines and mandated uniform ballot design and vote counting procedures. But, outside of Florida, there has been little effort to change the system of voting. Voting always has been in the hands of state and local officials, but the sense is that few states are eager to be the first to make expensive changes, and would rather wait for the federal government to give guidance and direction (and perhaps funds) to bring some clarity and uniformity to this hodge-podge system.

Third Party Candidates, often brushed aside as nuisance candidates, ideological crackpots, or big spending businessmen stroking their own egos, have to be taken seriously. Not necessarily their message or their platforms, but their impact on tight elections. Nader certainly was the third party candidate who had the most prominence. Yet, the Florida race was so close that had the 562 votes of last-place candidate James Harris of the Socialist Workers Party in Florida been cast for Al Gore, George W. Bush would have been denied the presidency. It is highly unlikely that any third party candidate would ever win the presidency, but they can, and did, gum up the results for the two major parties. Thus encouraged, the United States probably can expect to see more third party candidates in future presidential elections.

Supreme Court as Arbiter. The Court was put in an extraordinarily awkward position: its decision determined the outcome of the executive branch of government. The Court probably lost more in popular support and legitimacy when it precipitously stopped the Florida recount, and when it exposed its partisan and ideological raw nerves for the world to see. Many years and many elections will have to go by before the Supreme Court feels comfortable ruling again on the direct outcome of a presidential contest.

Electoral College Reform. The train wreck finally came. After 112 years and 14 presidential elections, the complicated equation of creating an electoral majority combined with a popular majority broke down. After early and vociferous calls for reform or abolition of the Electoral College, the issue faded quickly. The Electoral College, crafted two centuries ago for a vastly different political, cultural, and geographical landscape, has been transformed into a workable, albeit awkward, mechanism for Presidential selection.

There were two positive experiences out of this extraordinary election:

Great Civics Lesson. During the month of Florida recount controversy, Americans, transfixed to their televisions and logging on to political and news Internet sites at unprecedented rates, were engaged in a major civics lesson. Primarily, Americans learned about the bumpy mechanics of the Electoral College. They learned about recounts, the fundamental principle that every vote should be counted, and they learned about the tortuous path that ultimately led to the Supreme Court's final decision. At least for a month, there was a revitalized and renewed interest in politics and elections. For a country with less than 50 percent of its adult population bothering to show up for the country's most important election and with many completely turning away from politics and the political process, this renewed attention was a good sign. Politics meant something, every vote counted, and citizens relearned that they had a civic duty to participate. These great lessons may not have a lasting effect, but they at least for the moment raised important issues.

Graciously Accepting Defeat. With all that had transpired in Florida and the uncertainty and irregularities of the recount, it had to come as an extraordinary disappointment for Al Gore and his running mate Joseph Lieberman. Once the final decision had been announced by the Supreme Court, however, Gore accepted the decision with grace and dignity. There were no further political challenges, no attempted court fights, no threats of revenge, no demonstrations in the streets, and no manning of the barricades. The transition from one administration to the next was peaceful, filled with steady, reassuring symbolism as Al Gore congratulated George W. Bush while they stood on the rain-soaked dais on the west Capitol steps at the Inauguration ceremony.

In 2000, democracy prevailed. The electoral system, for all its short-comings, worked. But the 2000 elections also put America on notice that the important act of voting was a fragile and precious privilege, to be guarded against its own internal flaws.

REFERENCES

Associated Press. (2001). "Voter News Service Opts to Carry On, but Revamp." *The Washington Post*, June 1, A4.

Center for Responsive Politics Website. (*www.opensecrets.org/2000elect/other/bush*).

Johnson, Dennis W. (2001). *No Place for Amateurs: How Political Consultants Are Reshaping American Democracy*. New York: Routledge.

Kimberling, William C. (n.d.). "The Electoral College." Washington, D.C.: Federal Election Commission. (*www.fec.gov*).

Kurtz, Howard. (2000). "Errors Plagued Election Night Polling Services." *Washington Post*, December 22, A1.

Lavrakas, Paul J. and Jack K. Holley, eds. (1991). *Polling and Presidential Election Coverage*. Newbury Park, Calif.: Sage Publications.

Mintz, John and Peter Slevin. (2001). "Human Factor Was at Core of Vote Fiasco." *Washington Post*, June 2001, A1.

Powell, Michael. (2000). "Seared but Unwilted." *Washington Post*, December 27, C1.

Thomas, Evan et al. (1997). *Back from the Dead: How Clinton Survived the Republican Revolution*. New York: Atlantic Monthly Press.

Von Drehle, David, Jo Becker, Ellen Nakashima and Lois Romano. (2001). "A 'Queen' Kept Clock Running." *Washington Post*, January 30, A1.

Von Drehle, David, Peter Sleven, Dan Balz, and James V. Grimaldi. (2001a). "Anxious Moments in the Final Stretch." *Washington Post*, February 3, A1.

Who Pays the Piper?
The Funding of Political Campaigning
in the UK, US and the Consequences
for Political Marketing and Public Affairs

Phil Harris

Manchester Metropolitan University, UK

SUMMARY. This paper, using research from the UK and comparable US studies, looks at the growth in party fundraising, ethics of the process, impact on electoral systems, candidates, parties, campaigning and methods of obtaining funds (one donor in the UK has recently agreed to give £5million to the Conservative Party because they are anti EU whilst Labour gained £1million from the smoking lobby in 1997). It then links this to a growth in strategic public affairs and outlines the direct causal link between political lobbying and party fundraising. *[Article copies available for a fee from The Haworth Document Delivery Service: 1-800-HAWORTH. E-mail address: <getinfo@haworthpressinc.com> Website: <http://www.HaworthPress.com> © 2002 by The Haworth Press, Inc. All rights reserved.]*

Phil Harris is affiliated with The Centre for Corporate and Public Affairs at Manchester Metropolitan University Business School.

Address correspondence to: Dr. Phil Harris, Centre for Corporate and Public Affairs, Manchester Metropolitan University Business School, Aytoun Building, Aytoun Street, Manchester M1 3GH, England, UK (E-mail: P.harris@mmu.ac.uk or Website: www.man-bus.mmu.ac.uk/ccpa/index.htm).

[Haworth co-indexing entry note]: "Who Pays the Piper? The Funding of Political Campaigning in the UK, US and the Consequences for Political Marketing and Public Affairs." Harris, Phil. Co-published simultaneously in *Journal of Political Marketing* (The Haworth Political Press, an imprint of The Haworth Press, Inc.) Vol. 1, No. 2/3, 2002, pp. 89-107; and: *Communication of Politics: Cross-Cultural Theory Building in the Practice of Public Relations and Political Marketing* (eds: Bruce I. Newman, and Dejan Verčič) The Haworth Political Press, an imprint of The Haworth Press, Inc., 2002, pp. 89-107. Single or multiple copies of this article are available for a fee from The Haworth Document Delivery Service [1-800-HAWORTH, 9:00 a.m. - 5:00 p.m. (EST). E-mail address: getinfo@haworthpressinc.com].

10.1300/J199v01n02_07

KEYWORDS. Political campaigning, political marketing, public affairs, United Kingdom, United States

INTRODUCTION

The role and significance of political marketing in modern politics is widely debated, with political consultants, pundits and government bodies (Neill, 1998) arguing its increasing impact, whilst many politicians deny its effectiveness or relevance. If the latter is the case then it is surprising that the British Political parties spent over £50 million on campaigning in the 1997 General Election Campaign, whilst the US Presidential Campaign and associated campaigning of 2000 exceeded $3 billion in total expenditure (*Washington Post*, November 16th, 2000). Latest estimates suggest that in the UK a similar amount of expenditure was spent in 2001 as in 1997 a fall in real terms. Part of this is probably a result of the political parties having to spend money over a delayed and extended campaign period and diminished funds within the Conservative Party. There was supposed to be an electoral ceiling on expenditure, yet the new regulatory body in the area, the Electoral Commission has admitted it cannot police expenditure. What implications does this growing cost of election campaigning have on democratic politics? Who is funding this escalating cost and what are the implications for policy making? How is influence exerted and what conclusions can we draw for political marketing and public affairs are explored.

THE UNITED STATES OF AMERICA

The concept of political marketing originated in the United States (Cutlip, 1994; Kavanagh, 1995). Some writers see its beginnings in the 1950s and 1960s (Maarek, 1995; Beresford, 1998) or at the beginning of the century (McNair, 1996). It has been argued that political marketing became inevitable because of a mass electorate and development of the mass media (Harrop, 1990). According to Mareek (1995), the main factors responsible for the early development of the phenomenon in the US were the presidential system, the tradition of election for all public offices and rapid expansion of modern mass media. The US also provides a good example of early usage of typical marketing tools, such as direct mail, political advertising and publicity stunts in political communication (Rothschild, 1978; Melder, 1992; Newman, 1994 and 1999). More recently there has been increasing concerns raised at the scale and size of campaign funds and their impact on the democratic process, for instance, remonstrances by McCain after his unsuccessful bid for the Republican Presidential nomination (*Washington Post*, 25th June 2000).

US ELECTION EXPENDITURE

In Article I, section 4, and Article II, section 1, the US Constitution authorizes Congress to regulate federal elections. But, just as plainly, that regulation must conform to restraints imposed by the First Amendment to the Constitution. And here, the Supreme Court has said repeatedly that, under the First Amendment, campaign contributions and expenditures are protected speech.

Thus, more precisely, the Court has said that the regulation of political contributions and expenditures will be upheld only if they achieve a compelling governmental interest by the least restrictive means–the most difficult of constitutional hurdles. Recently, the Cato Institute published two studies–one by Professor Lillian R. BeVier of the University of Virginia School of Law, the other co-authored by attorneys Douglas Johnson of the National Right to Life Committee and Mike Beard of the Coalition to Stop Gun Violence–both of which concluded that campaign finance reform proposals put before Congress would not pass a constitutional vote.

Modern federal election campaign finance regulation stems from the Federal Election Campaign Act of 1971 (FECA), as amended in 1974. Two years later, in the landmark case of *Buckley v. Valeo*, the Supreme Court struck down many of the 1974 revisions as impermissible under the First Amendment.

Since then the Federal Election Commission (FEC) has fought to close the perceived "loopholes" created by Buckley. In response, the Court has repeatedly held that the First Amendment is not a loophole. Most recently, the Court held 7 to 2 in *Colorado Republican Federal Campaign Committee v. FEC* that independent expenditures by political parties cannot be limited by Congress. Then in April of this year, as if to underscore the long series of cases since Buckley, the Fourth Circuit took the extraordinary step of ordering the FEC to pay the legal fees incurred by the Christian Action Network in defending itself from an FEC lawsuit. Yet despite that string of cases, now spanning more than two decades, many in Congress persist in believing that they have the power to restrict what the First Amendment was plainly written and meant to protect. Thus, it is worth examining, if only in outline, just why the Constitution does not permit such restrictions.

In his June 3rd Outlook piece in the *Washington Post*, "It's Not Corruption, It's Politics," Peter J. Wallison argued that the Supreme Court should overturn the congressional limitation on what political parties can spend in coordination with their federal candidates. He said the current hard money limit on what an individual can give to a single party committee makes it "unlikely" that a contributor could unduly influence a candidate through a party contribution.

However, this $20,000 limit means that a couple can give $80,000 per two-year House election cycle or $240,000 per six-year Senate cycle to a national political party committee. Moreover, with the expanding range of fundraising schemes–such as bundling contributions, spousal tag teams, contributor swapping, joint fundraising programs and tally programs–no candidate or committee stands in isolation from others in the party.

Lawrence Noble, Executive Director of the Center for Responsive Politics, has found that financial, insurance and real estate sector was able to contribute more than $28 million in hard money to Republican National Party committees and more than $21 million to the Democratic National Party committees in the 1999-2000 election cycle.

Wallison also dismisses the massive soft money elephant sitting in the middle of the room. When soft and hard money contributions are added together, the same financial, insurance and real estate sector gave more than $89 million to the Republican National Party committees and more than $66 million to the Democratic National Party committees in the last election cycle.

If the Supreme Court does strike down the decades-old limit on what the party committees can spend in coordination with their candidates, it will only further allow the party committees to act as clearinghouses for the interests of those whose hard and soft money largess seems to know no bounds.

UNITED KINGDOM

In Britain, political marketing as a phenomenon acquired significance in the 1980s under the political party leaderships of Margaret Thatcher and Neil Kinnock who aimed to integrate all political communications and control the news agendas. However, it has also been suggested that major political parties have been engaged in marketing related activities for most of the twentieth century (Harrop, 1990;

Kavanagh, 1995; Wring, 1996). There has been a significant increase in focus on the packaging and presentation of leaders, partly due to the move of the Labour Party towards the centre right ground (Foley, 1993; Jones, 1995; Harris, Lock, and Roberts,1999) replicating Clinton Democrat positioning strategy.

As in the USA, television has the most significant impact on political communication and is the factor which dominates all other considerations by party strategists which is the battle to dominate the television agenda (Butler and Kavanagh, 1992; Crewe and Gosschalk, 1995; Scammell, 1995). These developments in campaign communications have resulted in the dramatic increase in the potential influence of the media (Norris, 1997b) and the demand for larger campaign funds.

Table 1 represents known centrally spent campaign funds as reported to the UK Committee of Standards in Public Life (Neill, 1998) by the political parties in 1997 and does not include the smaller or regional parties or regional expenditure; if these are taken into account, then 1997 expenditure would exceed £80 million.

CAMPAIGN EXPENDITURE
BY POLITICAL PARTIES IN THE UK

The Political Parties, Elections and Referendums Act 2000 for the first time introduced limits on campaign expenditure by political parties. The controls normally apply in the 365 days before the date of a general election, however, special arrangements apply to this election as the controls only came into force on 16 February 2001. The limits will apply to campaign expenditure incurred from that date to the date of the poll. The limit on expenditure applies to "qualifying expenses": these include expenses in respect of advertising, the production of party

TABLE 1. Expenditure by the Major UK Political Parties in the 1997 General Election

Political Party	Expenditure During Campaign
Labour Party	£25,700,000
Conservative Party	£28,300,000
Liberal Democrat Party	£2,300,000

Source: Neill of Bladen (1998)

election broadcasts, direct mail, the production of a manifesto, canvassing and election rallies.

The limit on what a party may spend is determined by the number of seats it contests. Parties in the 2001 Election received an allowance of £24,000 per constituency. Separate limits applied to expenditure in each of England, Scotland, Wales and Northern Ireland. A party that contests all constituencies in each part of the United Kingdom may, therefore, spend up to:

England (529 constituencies)	£12,696,000
Scotland (72 constituencies)	£1,728,000
Wales (40 constituencies)	£960,000
Northern Ireland (18 constituencies)	£432,000
Total	£15,816,000

Source: Electoral Commission 2001

Parties are required to submit a return to the Electoral Commission within three months of the date of the election or, if the total expenditure exceeds £250,000, within six months of the election. Where a party's expenditure exceeds £250,000 the return is required to be audited. A party that exceeds the limits on campaign expenditure is liable on conviction (on indictment) to an unlimited fine. The result of the election is unaffected by such a conviction.

DONATIONS TO POLITICAL PARTIES DURING THE ELECTION PERIOD

Under the Political Parties, Elections and Referendums Act 2000 political parties are required to submit a quarterly return to the Electoral Commission detailing donations it has accepted in excess of £5,000 (when received by the party's central organisation) or of £1,000 (when received by a constituency association or other sub-unit of the party). Donation reports must include the name and address of the donor and the precise amount of the donation. The reports are published by the Electoral Commission, although the addresses of individual donors are not disclosed.

During an election period–that is, the period beginning with the day on which Her Majesty's intention to dissolve Parliament is announced and ending with the date of the poll–parties are required to submit weekly donation reports. These weekly donation reports should detail donations in excess of £5,000 received by the central organisation of the party. A party has 30 days in which to decide whether to accept a donation. Consequently, the fact that a donation appears in a weekly donation report does not mean that the party has decided to accept a donation.

DONATIONS IN THE UK

The biggest ever single recorded donation to a British political party was reported in the Guardian Newspaper in May, ahead of the General Election campaign when the Conservative Party announced that they had received a £5m donation from a city betting entrepreneur. The money, from Stuart Wheeler, the 65-year-old head of the IG betting index, was said to come without strings and was prompted by his "admiration" for the Tory leader, William Hague. Who, post the election, is no more.

The move moved political parties another step away from funding by ordinary memberships and small-scale voluntary donations. Just after Christmas, Labour announced that it had received donations of £2m from millionaire publisher Lord Hamlyn and philanthropist Christopher Ondaatje. The party also received a promise of £2m from the science minister, Lord Sainsbury, towards its electoral campaign war chest.

The £5m donation came as a relief to the Conservatives, who have been short of funds from business and consequently over-dependent on their party treasurer, Lord Ashcroft. There is now an election expenditure ceiling in operation in the UK of £15m on election campaign spending, although this will be difficult to police. It is suspected that actual campaign expenditure will be similar to 1997, Mr. Wheeler's largesse will cover a third of the Conservatives' election expenditure.

Although the government is imposing a spending cap on election campaign expenditure, parties still badly need cash to run their day-to-day operations, as well as to fund pre-election campaigning, such as the poster campaign undertaken by the Conservatives.

Up until the 1997 election, the Tories managed to massively outspend Labour in elections with a regular bombardment of posters and newspaper adverts. The sheer scale of the Tory operation demoralised Labour. The size of Mr. Wheeler's gift, coupled with the trio of £2m donations to Labour, is bound to stimulate calls for the state funding of political parties. Tony Blair has said he is personally opposed to state funding, largely because he believes it would be politically unpopular. The third party in UK Politics the Liberal Democrats cannot compete with this scale of fundraising and consequently have regularly called for state funding of political campaigns both for practical and ethical reasons.

Mr. Wheeler started his firm with a £5,000 loan in 1974. The firm took tax-free bets on the price of gold, and since then the business has diversified into all the leading commodities, stock indices and sport. The recent addition of betting on individual shares allowed the firm to treble annual profits to £10.1m. The company also takes bets on politics. When the company floated in July on the stock market shares were 240p. Since then the price has more than doubled.

In 1998 the company's Internet division launched the first site to offer online spread betting and that has become one of its main arms. Last year turnover rose 58% to £15.8m. Despite his faith in the Tories, Mr. Wheeler is a shrewd gambler and in the last election put his money on the Labour party. He is also a former finalist in the world poker championships.

Mr. Wheeler is also on the National Council of Business for Sterling, the anti-Euro campaign body.

LOBBYIST SUPPORT FOR UK POLITICAL PARTIES

The Guardian newspaper has reported that the Labour Party has also become much more attached to the Lobbyists. At 7:30 a.m. most days during the election campaign Colin Byrne, chief executive of the public relations consultancy Weber Shandwick Worldwide, had a meeting with Clive Hollick, chief executive of United News and Media plc, at Labour's headquarters at Millbank. Hollick heads the party's business relations unit and Byrne has been working closely with him–"in a personal capacity and outside of working hours," as he puts it–to persuade the corporate sector to support Labour.

The work culminated in a letter of support from chief executives to the Times and in the party's business manifesto, which promised to make mergers and takeovers easier.

Byrne, himself a former deputy PR director at Millbank, is a key figure in the interface between big business and New Labour. His company, owned by the US giant Interpublic Inc., represents such clients as the advertising agency Adshel and Tesco, which have sponsored party events.

Byrne is not the only lobbyist to have worked for Labour during the election. So was his former boss, David Hill, a senior executive at

Bell-Pottinger Communications and managing director of Good Relations ltd., which represented Monsanto. Labour's communications director from 1991 until 1999 and close to Tony Blair, Hill has also acted for Securicor Custodial Services which bids for government contracts in the prison service. "I have taken unpaid leave," he says.

Alongside Hill in the Millbank was Ceri Evans, former adviser to William Hague, campaign manager for Steve Norris during his bid to be mayor of London and now managing director of the lobbyists Golin Harris Ludgate.

Millbank insiders were uneasy about the presence of these lobbyists during the campaign. Although they say they are "taking unpaid leave," these consultants are in effect working for Labour for free. Political Lobbyists like Byrne and Hill charge clients up to £225 per hour (Lord Bell, the Tory PR strategist and Hill's boss, charges up to £750 per hour.) If they have been working at Millbank for three weeks, then the party is benefiting from tens of thousands of pounds of staff not paid fees.

As Labour has not declared this benefit-in-kind, some lobbyists believe that it could be in breach of the new Political Parties Funding Act. The Association of Professional Political Consultants (APPC) is conducting an inquiry and has approached the Electoral Commission, the independent body set up to monitor political donations, for guidance. The commission seems confused. It told the APPC that such secondment could be a political payment: "Donations and campaign expenditure may be incurred where a company provides the services of an employee to a political party." It says paid "special leave," too, would constitute a donation.

But the commission also thinks that "the provision by any individual of his own services which he provides voluntarily in his own time and free of charge is not to be regarded as a donation."

The APPC is not satisfied and has commissioned a further legal opinion. For there is no doubt that a highly paid, experienced lobbyist working for free is a financial benefit to a political party.

Labour is not unique in benefiting from free expertise from lobbyists. During the Conservative administration of 1983-1987, Lord Bell, then chief executive of Lowe Howard-Spink, seconded one of his consultants, Howell James, to be special adviser to Lord Young in the Cabinet Office while continuing to pay his salary. And then, when Lord Young became DTI secretary, he received the benefit of Peter Luff (now a Tory MP) as a free special adviser—again courtesy of Lord Bell's firm.

But now we have seen large numbers of political consultants being based in a party HQ trying to help the party of government be re-elected. Byrne and Hill, however, "unpaid," remain managing directors of lobbying corporations. So their expertise and connections are of commercial value when they were at Millbank.

MAKING SENSE OF INFLUENCE

If one looks at campaign funding and associated activity it is very clear from my own research into party conferences in the UK that there is direct linkage between political lobbying and party campaign funding. This I see as inevitable and needs regulation. It also is one the route causes for a growing interest in public affairs research. Let's try and make sense now of how the process of influence and lobbying is evolving as part of the modern democratic process.

GROWTH OF LOBBYING

Lobbying has grown considerably in the past fifteen years in the UK, which was outlined in the factors discussed earlier. Precise information on the current scale of activity is hard to come by, the first Nolan Report notwithstanding, due to the difficulty of choosing what to measure and the general discretion in the way in which lobbying has to be conducted. However, there is substantial evidence of its dramatic increase (Harris and Lock, 1996). The growth of corporate lobbying and campaigning is a response to the complexities of modern business society caused by more pervasive government and increased need for competitiveness in a global market by companies. Harris and Lock (1996) reported estimates that expenditure on commercial political lobbying, both in-house and by independent lobbyists, in the UK was between 200 and 300 million pounds and that over 4,000 people were directly employed in this activity. It was also estimated that expenditure at EU level was at least one order of magnitude greater than at national level. Recent evidence suggests that political lobbying in the EU is worth over £3 billion (source author's informant).

BUSINESS SITUATIONS
IN WHICH LOBBYING PLAYS A ROLE

I propose below a taxonomy of situations in which government is involved and postulate the relative importance of lobbying in influencing outcomes:

1. Government as Purchaser or Allocator

a. Winner takes all.
In a number of situations, there is only one contract or opportunity to be bid for. A recent example is Camelot's successful bid to run the National Lottery. TV franchises, the Channel Tunnel consortium and certain military contracts have similar characteristics. Price is rarely the sole criterion. The public decision is usually very visible and lobbying is rife.

b. Large, infrequent contracts.
Defence and large public works contracts are typical of this category. Increasingly failure to obtain such contracts threatens the very existence of the company or a strategic business unit with a visible and politically delicate impact on employment. The situation of ABB's railway works interests is one example. Again lobbying plays an important role.

c. Regularly supplied items.
Apart from highly specialised items, these are usually supplied through standard purchasing procedures, notably by competitive tender. These procedures leave little scope for lobbying, except in so far as it may be necessary to qualify a supplier to be included in the approved list or to pass any other pre-tender hurdles.

2. Government as Legislator and Framer of Regulations

Legislation on matters such as product safety, trademarks and intellectual property, and fair trading are obvious targets for business lobbying to ensure that legitimate interests are protected. However, it is easily forgotten that a great deal of matters that affect specific businesses are enacted through regulations under enabling legislation. Visible examples are vehicle construction and use regulations, and regulations affecting food and agriculture. Lobbying is important here to ensure that regulations are sensibly framed and represent an appropriate balance of business and other pressure group interests.

3.   Government as Initiator of Action

There are a number of explicit circumstances in which the relevant secretary of state initiates action by a quango or similar
body. The most familiar case is the Monopolies and Mergers
Commission. In other examples, where a quango can initiate action itself, the government of the day exerts some influence in
terms of matters that are taken up and is frequently the final arbiter in terms of action upon the recommendations it receives.
Lobbying in terms of provision of information as well as persua-
sive communication play an important role in shaping the prog-
ress of events.

4.   Government and European Legislation and Regulation

In Europe with the increasing influence of European directives and
regulations upon product markets, proper representation of manufacturers' and marketers' interests have become critical in those areas which the EU is seeking to regulate. As well as direct lobbying
of Commission officials and MEPs and representation through
pan-European business bodies, support from one's own national
government through civil servants and the Council of Ministers is
critical to success on significant issues. In these instances, lobbying
at both national and EU level is an essential activity.

5.   Government as Decision Maker

There are a range of other situations where the government has
de facto or de jure powers to take decisions, which affect business. Whilst the example is not directly a marketing one, the recent controversy over the decision to permit Shell to sink the
Brent Spar platform in the Atlantic is a good illustration, both of
convincing government of the correctness of a course of action,
and also of a failure of a broader public relations campaign
against a more well-organised, but less well-funded opponent.

FUTURE DIRECTIONS

The author has just recently conducted research with members of
both UK houses of Parliament and Whitehall officials and what clearly

emerges is that organisations can be seriously disadvantaged, if they are not providing information to support their long-term business positions or counter their national and international corporate competitors by providing information to relevant bodies. This may well sound very logical, but the reality is that a number of interests and companies do not know how or understand the various UK and EU government processes and their ability to develop policy and regulations which impact upon them and the markets in which they operate. This puts them at a serious disadvantage.

MODERN MACHIAVELLIAN MARKETING

Increasingly, to be able to compete means being able to exert pressure on government to gain competitive edge. Let me give some examples of EU government areas where if one can change views of government, one can gain advantage. A well-argued case, which has been outlined before, is that it has been suggested that a number of German and French car manufacturers successfully lobbied the EU for them to adopt catalytic converters as their preferred vehicle emissions measures. This became compulsory legislation, to the advantage of Mercedes, Audi, VW and Peugeot et al. At a stroke this wiped out one billion pounds worth of investment by Ford in lean burn engine technology and half million pounds investment by Austin Rover, also developing this technology. Both Ford and Austin Rover deemed this technology to be a lot cleaner than just using catalytic converters. They had opted to go for a higher specification system rather than the intermediate catalytic converters. Once the legislation was enacted across the EU, Ford lost its billion pound investment in R and D and had to reinvest in catalytic converters to catch up. Austin Rover, as a result of this policy, lost its investment, could never catch up and went bankrupt. BMW now own Austin Rover.

The second example is that Philip Morris are probably spending in the order of at least 50 million pounds a year in Brussels trying to stop national states and the EU bringing in similar measure for compensation to meet health care risks of cancer infected tobacco smokers. The money is being used to delay legislation, which leads to compulsory care and compensation for sufferers. In the States, it is now almost mandatory for many to get care for tobacco related diseases. By delaying the legislation Philip Morris benefits financially.

Other areas where one can exert pressure to lobby for advantage are:

Packaging. Which may use only particular materials across Europe to meet specifications. Clearly this disadvantages its competitive edge to certain processes and companies.

Broadcasting. As broadcasting internationalises the granting of licences or privatisation of public broadcasting can give strategic advantages. Look at Murdoch or Time Warner.

Health. Delays in environmental protection, tobacco legislation or alcohol abuse have an effect both on the healthcare industry and certain businesses.

Travel/Ecology. Restricting travel and tourism may benefit the ecology or may just mean that if you have the money then you can go there.

Resources. Clearly, the allocation of fossil fuels, emissions and scarce resources and their availability also impact on competitive edge. Reliable and renewable electricity can give competitive advantage. Erratic and hazardous energy systems can lead to decline. People do not shop in Chernobyl any more.

THE RISE OF REGULATION

Lobbying has grown as a result of business and non-governmental organisations wishing to influence government regulatory policy. As government has sold its ownership of control of various sectors of the economy—utilities, broadcasting, etc.—so it has tried to shake the direction of these now private companies or organisations and their interests through regulation. In fact the last part of the 20th Century and early part of the 21st Century has seen government at every level develop the regulator and regulation. To influence that regulation leads to strategic gain for the organisation. If you can shape the market to your advantage then you win and lobbying is about shaping that regulation so that it suits you and your interests. I have developed throughout my research a number of core graphs to indicate graphically how one exerts pressure. The first one is called the Machiavellian graph and shows that each time government increases regulation, lobbying public affairs activity increases to shape that regulation (see Figure 1).

This can also be graphically shown in a 2 × 2 matrix, which I called the Machiavellian matrix, the more government regulatory policy, the higher the level of lobbying, thus intense activity (see Figure 2).

We can see this being developed further if we look at the ways in which business, lobbying and policies can be used to influence government in the following model of influencing decision making at the national and transnational government levels (see Figure 3).

CONCLUSION

As ever, Machiavelli provides a useful guide to exploring government and where to exert influence. There has been a growth in lobbying because as government has withdrawn from its role of being owner in the economy it has attempted to regulate and set the business environment for companies to operate in. However, the more competitive com-

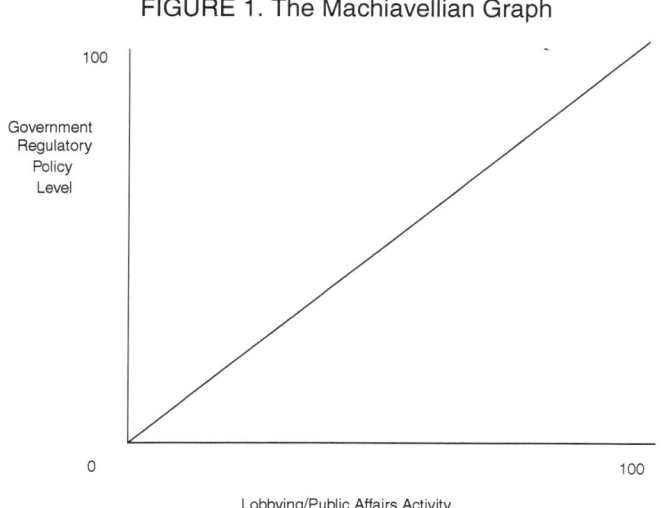

FIGURE 1. The Machiavellian Graph

FIGURE 2. The Machiavellian Marketing Matrix (The Isotropic Relationship Between Market Share and Levels of Political Lobbying: The Maintenance of a Dominant or Monopolistic Position in a Market Sector Through Political Lobbying)

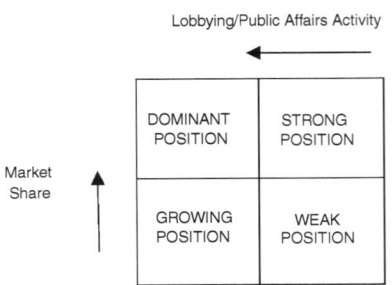

parties and NGOs influence that regulation to their own competitive advantage. There are currently 28,000 NGOs registered in Brussels explicitly just to influence EU policy. I wonder why?

Lobbying is part of modern political communication. As politicians become increasingly isolated and short of quality information, effective lobbying fills up that vacuum and allows good decision making (and of course some times bad decision making). Globalisation is meaning that to gain competitive edge transnationally, lobbying is used to influence the EU, the WTO, NATA, etc.

In the UK the need for parties to raise large amounts of funding with no regulation of activity has led to certain individuals acting as millionaire sugar daddies to parties (see Appendix 1: Large Donation News). One assumes these special relationships have their consequences.

A trend is of course accountability and lobbying has to be seen to account like government and be of a high ethical standard and interests declared. As society has higher demands, so it will want its voices heard and society will become more consumer driven and government will have to become more responsive to consumer needs. Perhaps consumer needs would be better roads, better health care, better education, rather than some of the things that politicians in the past have wanted. Consumers need to lobby for that quality of life and for resources to be spent on priority areas. All that we can say is that we can be sure of one thing, that as government increasingly develops a regulatory society, so lobbying will grow and the only way to counter this is if your voice is heard.

FIGURE 3. The Role of Political Lobbying as a Feature of Political Marketing Communication with Government: A Model

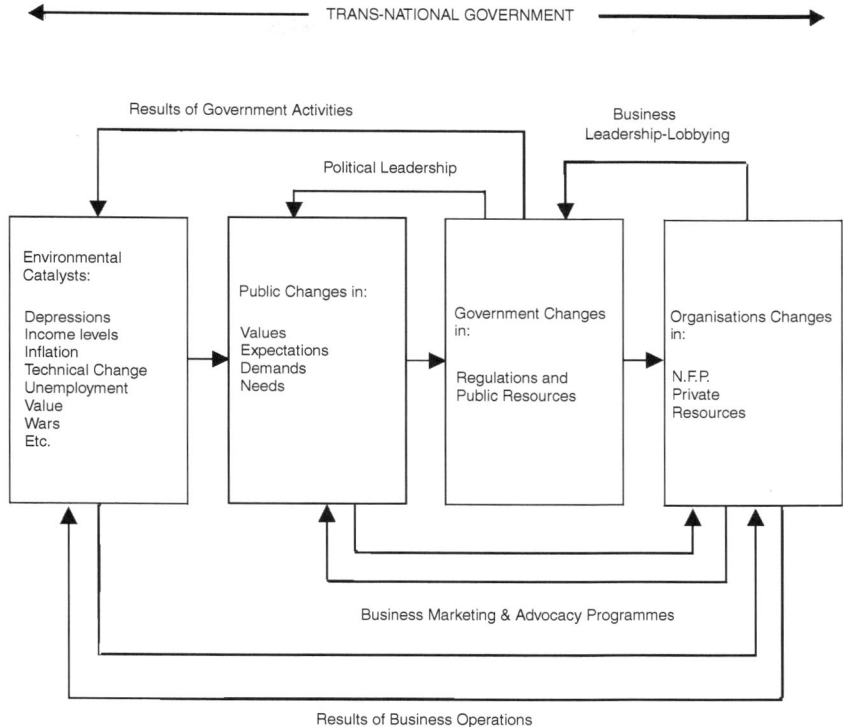

All armed prophets conquered, All the unarmed perished

Nicollo Machiavelli (Harris, Lock and Rees, 2000)

REFERENCES

Barnett, A. and Bright, M. In *The Sunday Observer*, 10th June, London 2000.

Beresford, Q. (1998). Selling democracy short: Elections in the age of the market. Current Affairs Bulletin. 74 (5): 24-32.

Butler, D. and Kavanagh, D. (1992). Electioneering: A Comparative Study of Continuity and Change. Oxford, Clarendon Press.

Crewe, I. and Gosschalk, B. (eds.). (1995). Political Communications: The General Election Campaign of 1992. Cambridge, Cambridge University Press.

Cutlip, M., Center, A.H., and Broom, G.L. (1994). Effective Public Relations. Upper Saddle River, NJ, Prentice-Hall.

Electoral Commission 2001, see (*www.electoral-commission.gov.uk*). February 2002.

Foley, M. (1993). The Rise of the British Presidency. Manchester, Manchester University Press.

Harris, P. and Lock, A. (1996). Machiavellian Marketing: The development of corporate lobbying in the UK. *Journal of Marketing Management*, 12, 313-28.

Harris, P., Lock, A., and Rees, P. (eds.). 2000. Machiavelli, Marketing and Management. London, Routledge.

Harris, P., Lock, A., and Roberts, J. (1999). Limitations of political marketing? A content analysis of press coverage of political issues during the 1997 UK General Election campaign. In B. Newman (ed.), *Handbook of Political Marketing*. Thousand Oaks, CA, Sage.

Harrop, M. (1990). Political Marketing. In *Parliamentary Affairs*, London, 43, 277-92.

Jones, N. (1995). Soundbites and Spin Doctors. London, Cassell.

Kavanagh, D. (1995). Election Campaigning: The New Marketing of Politics. Oxford: Blackwell.

Maarek, P. (1995). *Political Marketing and Communication*. London: John Libbey & Co.

McNair, B. (1996). Performance in politics and the politics of performance. In J. L'Etang, and M. Pieczka (eds.), *Critical Perspectives in Public Relations*. London: Thomson Learning.

Melder, K. (1992). Hail to the Candidate, Presidential campaigns from Banners to Broadcasts. London: Smithsonian Institute.

Neil of Bladen. (1998). Fifth Report of the Committee on Standards in Public Life: The funding of Political Parties in the United Kingdom, Vol. 1 and 2. CM 4057-1. London, TSO.

Newman B. (1994). The Marketing of the President. Thousand Oaks, CA: Sage.

Newman, B. (ed.). (1999). The Handbook of Political Marketing. Thousand Oaks, CA: Sage.

Norris, P. (1997). Electoral Change since 1945. Oxford, Blackwell.

Rayner, J. In *The Sunday Observer*, 17th June, London 2001.

Rothschild, M. (1978). Political advertising: A neglected policy issue in marketing. *Journal of Marketing Research* 15, 59-71.

Scammell, M. (1995). Designer Politics: How Elections are Won. London, Macmillan.

Wallison, P.J. 'It's Not Corruption, It's Politics.' *Washington Post*, June 3rd. Washington Post, November 16th, 2000.

APPENDIX 1

LARGE DONATION NEWS

THE HONORARY ENGLISHMAN: JOHN PAUL GETTY Jr.

Born American but now British, he longs for Orwell's lost England of warm beer and cricket. Last week he topped years of giving millions to unpopular causes with a £5million donation to the Tories.

Anybody trying to understand the millionaire philanthropist John Paul Getty Junior could do worse than look at the aims and priorities of the charity which holds both his name and a fair chunk of his money. The J. Paul Getty Jr. Charitable Trust is, according to its own literature, dedicated to funding "unpopular causes." Last week the depth of Getty's deep commitment to those ignored by society was finally revealed. It was announced that, the day before their disastrous election defeat, he had given the Conservative Party a £5 million donation.

On Thursday night the ailing 69-year-old Getty, who now requires dialysis twice a week and often has need of a wheelchair, spent another £1m on a more obvious cause: himself. He held a fabulous party, attended by just 500 of his closest friends. Mick Jagger and Camilla Parker Bowles were there. Jeremy Irons, Marianne Faithful and William Hague were on the guest list. Flaming torches flickered on the driveway, as guests arrived by hired luxury coaches, sipping the champagne they had been given for the journey.

Getty has not explained the reason for the bash. Maybe, with his health failing, he wanted a final fling. Then again, perhaps there was something about that one fat cheque to the Tories which was worth celebrating. It stands as final proof that a long, almost desperate process of reinvention, is now complete. In 1998 he handed back his American passport and took British citizenship. He has developed an obsession with cricket and, at his Buckinghamshire estate, built perhaps the best pitch in the country which draws to it the world's greatest players.

The Sunday Observer, 17th June, Jay Rayner.

TYCOON FACES QUIZ OVER POLITICAL DONATIONS

The British Iraqi-born tycoon, Nadhmi Auchi, who is wanted for questioning in France over his alleged role in the Elf-Aquitaine scandal, has given thousands of pounds in political donations in the UK, *The Observer* can reveal.

Last year French judges issued an arrest warrant for Auchi and started extradition proceedings against the billionaire businessman who is Britain's seventh richest man. So far, the British government has rejected the extradition request. Auchi insists that he is innocent of any wrongdoing and happy to answer any questions in Britain from the French investigators.

The Sunday Observer, 10th June, Antony Barnett and Martin Bright.

Communicative Diplomacy
for the 3rd Millennium:
Soft Power
of Small Countries Like Slovenia?

Kristina Plavšak

University of Ljublijana, Slovenia

SUMMARY. In today's world of revolution in communications and information as well as of global interdependency, a medialised politics became a general reality. One can observe such a trend specifically in the field of international and foreign affairs where state and other actors use communication channels and public relations to a large extent to improve on the content and in particular, on the image of their policies. Here one can also argue that a major share of bilateral and multilateral relations among states is shaped by the international media, or vice versa, that all major "wars" are "fought" through the media.

This article explores the increasing inter-relation between state foreign affairs on one side, and media and public relations, on the other. The article starts off with basic concepts of a "new/democratic diplomacy" (Nicholson, 1988) and a "public diplomacy" (Signitzer in Combs, 1992), and compares them with definitions of "international public relations"

Kristina Plavšak, MIA, is affiliated with the Faculty of Social Sciences in the Department of Communication Studies in the Center for International Relations at the University of Ljubljana (E-mail: kristina.plavsak@uni-lj.si).

[Haworth co-indexing entry note]: "Communicative Diplomacy for the 3rd Millennium: Soft Power of Small Countries Like Slovenia?" Plavšak, Kristina. Co-published simultaneously in *Journal of Political Marketing* (The Haworth Political Press, an imprint of The Haworth Press, Inc.) Vol. 1, No. 2/3, 2002, pp. 109-122; and: *Communication of Politics: Cross-Cultural Theory Building in the Practice of Public Relations and Political Marketing* (eds: Bruce I. Newman, and Dejan Verčič) The Haworth Political Press, an imprint of The Haworth Press, Inc., 2002, pp. 109-122. Single or multiple copies of this article are available for a fee from The Haworth Document Delivery Service [1-800-HAWORTH, 9:00 a.m. - 5:00 p.m. (EST). E-mail address: getinfo@haworthpressinc.com].

10.1300/J199v01n02_08

(Kunczik, 1997). It attempts to build the general analytical framework on the basis of comparative case studies of developed countries with an established diplomatic tradition and of new democracies still proving themselves on the international fora. In this context, particular attention is given to communication in relation to international organisations like NATO and the EU. *[Article copies available for a fee from The Haworth Document Delivery Service: 1-800-HAWORTH. E-mail address: <getinfo@haworthpressinc. com> Website: <http://www.HaworthPress.com> © 2002 by The Haworth Press, Inc. All rights reserved.]*

KEYWORDS. Democratic diplomacy, media diplomacy, media relations, public diplomacy, public relations

Diplomacy is entrusted to manage relations between states and between states and other actors, by advising, shaping and implementing foreign policy, articulating, co-ordinating and securing particular and wider interests.[1] In the "media shaped" world it adopts new dimensions, being concerned with media and communication management, and as some argue, developing to a genuine "communicative action."[2] With the trends of the information society a modern diplomat takes on a specific role of a public relations officer, a manager and a co-ordinator.[3] Further on, one predicts that the diplomacy of the future will be increasingly public, networked, technology-driven and electronic, and, therefore, education and training programmes for professional diplomats will work even more in these directions, towards specialisation in communication knowledge and skills.[4]

This article intends to explore the increasing inter-relation between state foreign affairs and diplomacy on one side, and media and public relations, on the other, as they started off in distinctly separate spheres and with different logic, but they seem to converge more and more. How foreign policy and diplomacy in the 3rd millennium actually work as one often perceives it as merely a simplified, popular presentation of events, meetings, issues, nicely wrapped up in an infotainment package and played out for the TV cameras? One would also like to see how the profession of a diplomat develops under such circumstances, and how it takes on media and public relations assignments. At the same time one would like to ask what these current trends bring to a small country like Slovenia and how should Slovene diplomats adapt to a communication society.

The paper will start off with basic concepts of an open, democratic diplomacy and a public diplomacy, linking them with the emergence of international public relations. Further on, it will analyse the trends of media diplomacy, medialised foreign policy and media wars. In conclusion the author will discuss the implications for the Slovene diplomacy within the described trends.

OPEN, DEMOCRATIC DIPLOMACY

The shift from a traditional (secret) diplomacy to its new, open and democratic forms can be traced back to the end of the World War I. The conclusions of the Conference in Brest Litovsk after the October revolution in Russia (1917) and the declaration of President's Woodrow Wilson 14 points at the Paris Peace Conference (1918) were the breaking points in this respect. Taking distance from previous practices of secret agreements among monarchs and privileged elites, these introduced a concept of an *open diplomacy*. As summarised in the words of Wilson: "open covenants of peace openly arrived at, after which there shall be no private international understandings of any kind" (Nicolson, 1988: 43). Here one argues that Wilsonian dictum was often mis-understood as it would be impossible and also unwise to conduct negotiations openly. Only the fact that the negotiations are taking place must, barring exceptional cases, be publicly known, and the results of the negotiations must also be publicly announced (Rangarajan, 1998: 21). At this point diplomacy ran into a contradiction which had to be solved in real life: as one became increasingly aware that public had to be involved somehow, diplomacy adapted to the new circumstances, thus, still it had to preserve a certain level of secrecy and closure to enable it to perform its professional function (Vukadinoviæ, 1994: 39).

The overall transformation of the "nature and spirit" of the traditional diplomacy entailed the whole democratic trends of the 19th century. *A democratic diplomacy* functioned according to the basic logic of the democratic parliamentary system: diplomat as a civil servant is subject to the Foreign Minister, who as a member of the Parliament is subject to the majority in the Parliament, and Parliament as a representative Assembly is subject to the will of the sovereign people. All in all, at that historic point it was stated and accepted that statesmen in their foreign policy performance and diplomats in their activity were bound to a democratic control of the people and, therefore, had to provide for a certain transparency and also flexibility of their action (Nicolson, 1988: 41-46).

Hence, it is stressed that the electoral process itself represents the institutionalisation of public opinion in international relations. As in democratic societies foreign policy makers and diplomats became more and more related to the electorates and respectively, sensitive to public attitudes, public opinion took on a special role and comprehension in the field of foreign affairs and diplomacy.[5] It was recognised as an important power even earlier on, described by Metternich as "a malevolent meteor hurled by divine providence upon Europe" or by Canning as "a power more tremendous than was perhaps ever yet brought to action in the history of mankind" (Nicolson, 1988: 37). However, one warned of particular difficulties with public opinion as related to the formulation and implementation of foreign policy: the sovereign people are not wholly aware of their responsibilities; they do not have sufficient knowledge about the state of foreign affairs and particular issues; and they are primarily interested in domestic matters. As to such a view, democratic diplomacy was facing dangers of being delayed in its execution and of being imprecise in its formulation, which both could be damaging its basic efficiency and effectiveness. In addition, with the acknowledgement of the role by the free press, democratic diplomacy attempted to balance between the demands for publicity and needs for discretion (Nicolson, 1988: 46-50).

The changes in the concept of diplomacy and its relation to the public altogether called for additional tasks of foreign service and diplomats. First and foremost, if the people were to exert democratic control over foreign policy, but not to obstruct its efficiency and effectiveness, one had to provide them with essential facts in digestible form. Here one stressed that work with the press was necessary, and abroad a new diplomatic post of a Press Attaché was conceived to carry out activities to this purpose. These were to maintain contacts with the local media, important opinion leaders and correspondents from home country, secure that the views of one's country are made public and that they obtain adequate publicity (Nicolson, 1988: 91). Furthermore, one already pointed to the possibility that press could be used to one's advantage, as a tool of persuasion or even propaganda. Such efforts to manipulate media coverage of foreign actors, events and policy issues were even more likely to succeed as foreign affairs were generally unobtrusive, i.e., the public was unlikely to have any direct experience with them, and information gathering about such issues was difficult (Manheim and Albritton, 1984: 643).

PUBLIC DIPLOMACY

Through further expansion of communication technology and broader public participation in the process of foreign affairs, diplomacy became more and more tied down to international media and public opinion. In its democratic, public role diplomacy broadened its scope of action to include diverse spheres of life, not merely "high politics," to involve, besides officials and professionals, also other relevant actors, and to open up to various foreign publics. It attempted to strengthen the efficiency and effectiveness of one's foreign policy by means of a systematic, multi-fold communication. It expanded its functions within the concept of *public diplomacy*, defined as "the way in which both government and private individuals and groups influence directly or indirectly those public attitudes and opinion which bear directly another government's foreign policy decision" (Signitzer and Coombs, 1992: 138).

Whereas traditional diplomacy was based on formal relations between governments or government-to-government communication, today governments speak and listen directly to the people also in other countries. In its efforts, public diplomacy is designed to bypass the constraints of foreign governments and reach directly into the hearts and minds of foreign audiences. Public diplomacy activities include, for example, government video teleconferences for journalists, students and other interest groups, or student/cultural and international visitors' exchanges (Alexandre, 1987: 30). Hereby, public diplomacy becomes an ever-widening arena that encompasses non-governmental organisations, multinational corporations, regional and local governments, academic institutions, media and other important players. Therefore, also "the actors in public diplomacy can no longer be confined to the profession of diplomats but include various individuals, groups and institutions who engage in international and intercultural communication activities which do have a bearing on the political relationships between two countries" (Signitzer and Coombs, 1992: 139).

One can trace similarities with the public relations: pursuing common aims of influencing public opinion to advantages of one's organisation/ government, targeting various groups in other countries, strategically planning for diplomatic (communication) activities, etc. Public diplomacy strives for intensive exchange of information, neutralisation of clichés and prejudices about one's nation, popularisation of one's foreign policy and social system, strengthening of one's country positive image. As such, its efforts overlap with *the international public relations*, defined as "a planned and organized effort of a company, institutior. or government to establish mutually beneficial relations with publics of other nations" (Wilcox et al., 1992; Grunig, 1993: 143) or "efforts to improve the image of one's country in foreign country (-ies) by distribution of interest motivating information" (Kunczik, 1993: 1). Both, public diplomacy and international public relations can work efficiently together toward rationalisation and synergy in transmission of relevant information about one's state and foreign policy. Thereby, they can complement each other in state promotion activities, by using "soft" methods of media and public relations, on one side and on the other, also "hard" methods of persuasion and propaganda, more or less covered in subtle forms of cultural, education, promotion, etc., programmes.

Nevertheless, public diplomacy is not merely a technique of state promotion, its basic content and quality is formulated and implemented foreign policy which cannot be merely compensated by means of public relations and advertising. The most important roles are played by credible and competent foreign affairs speakers who are involved with the policy decision making process. Efficient public diplomacy, responding in one voice, needs a strategic planning (recognition and solutions to open questions) and a systemic co-ordination of actors at the home Foreign Ministry, at embassies abroad and the other involved.[6] Apart from official contacts with the host government, modern diplomats nurture relations with diverse opinion makers and multiplicators, important and interesting people from all walks of life. They work more and more in co-operation with media, not against or in competition with them, and in addition, they take on the task of persistent convincing with relevant arguments, in public and in the media.[7]

MEDIA DIPLOMACY

What is a modern diplomat's role in the times when "unmediated dialogue and information exchange between citizens from around the world occurs 24 hours a day" (Wriston, 1997; Rothkopf, 1998: 328) and as "the media are increasingly a part of the process (if not the entire process) in the communication between governments and publics about international politics" (Karl, 1982: 144; Kunczik, 1993: 169)? The intense dynamics of media coverage in the last decade can be barely followed by the capabilities of foreign affairs actors to gather information, make a proper decision and inform the public on time. The story of the former Director of Communication to former President Clinton, George Stephanopoulos about how himself, the National Security advisor and the President got to know about anti-Yeltsin coup in Summer 1996 from the CNN first, is more than illustrative under the heading "once again CNN beat the CIA" (Stephanopoulos, 1999: 212). In a similar way, NATO's spokesman Jamie Shea explains: "The ability of the media to dramatise events and create a global audience for a conflict puts policy makers under pressure to take decisions faster and with less time for reflection than at any previous time in human history" (Shea, 1999: 5).

International television networks like CNN bring about "the constitution of a worldwide homogeneously time-zoned bios politikon, instantaneously affecting world wide political action or interaction via press conferences or public resolutions transmitted around the world" (Volkner, 1999: 3; Thussu, 2000: 12). The world leaders and diplomats are aware that CNN became an independent force in international politics and an important opinion leader by itself and often acts, as formulated by previous UN Secretary General Boutros Boutros-Ghali, in the seat of "the 16th member of the Security Council." Therefore, they strive to take on its advantages or the so-called "CNN effect," i.e., televise its foreign policy and sell it to the public (Thussu, 2000: 13). For example, these attempts were made by US Presidents from the early 1970s on: Nixon carefully choreographed his visit to China for prime-time viewing back home, Carter's administration engaged in "verbal ping-pong" with Tehran, sending messages back and forth via the TV channels, Reagan converted "photo ops" into a science in his foreign visits (Gergen, 1991: 47). Clinton mastered the medium, sending carefully staged TV pictures of foreign affairs events, like a historic shake hand between Palestinian leader Jaser Arafat and Israeli Prime Minister Barak on the White House lawn (Stephanopoulos, 1999).

Even with extreme measures, use of force, and when leading a war, one is more or less involved with the media presentation and interpretation, and faces a particular phenomenon of *media wars*. In today's conflicts political leaders spend as much time explaining or justifying a conflict to their public opinion and to the media as they actually do running them. Thus, as stressed by communication lessons of the NATO intervention on FRY, one has to keep in control: "Leaders have to dominate the media and not be dominated by it. Successful conflicts cannot be media driven. Winning the media campaign is just as important as winning the military campaign" (Shea, 1999: 8). Furthermore, one realises that "the realpolitik of the new era is cyberpolitik" in which the actors are no longer just states and raw power can be counted or fortified by information power. Internet technologies enable virtual communities to unite to counter government efforts, from use of violence to the closing off of existing media channels. These take their cases to the international court of public opinion, whose influence over states has grown as its means to reach an ever greater audience has multiplied. A world-wide network is the key feature of the environment in which diplomats and generals operate (Rothkopf, 1997: 325-330).

In this new democratic, media- and communication-driven environment, diplomacy not merely adapted to work with the media hand-in-hand, but also learned how to manipulate the media, stepping toward a more active involvement and management of media and communication to one's own country's purposes and advantages guided by national interests. With the emergence of a so-called *media diplomacy* and even *medialised foreign policy,* foreign policy decisions and diplomatic activity are more and more presented in news formats, also by pseudo-events and personification (Kunczik, 1993: 169). Furthermore, "Western diplomacy has become sophisticated in packaging public information in a visually astute fashion and television networks, which often operate in a symbiotic relationship with authorities, tend to conform the geo-political agendas set by powerful governments" (Thussu, 2000: 5). To this point, during the Rambouillet talks between Serbian leaders and Kosovo Albanians in February 1999, it was indeed metaphoric to see the exhausted faces of James Rubin, Spokesman of the State Department, and Christiane Amanpour, Chief Correspondent at CNN, in their private lives the happily married "Hollywood" couple, but each doing one's job on the opposite sides of the fence.

Even government officials and PR experts are critical of themselves in this respect: "What too often counts is how well the policy will 'play,' how the pictures will look, whether the right signals are being sent, and whether the public will be impressed by the swiftness of the government's response–not whether the policy promotes America's long-term interests" (Gergen, 1991: 48-49). Some scholars argue that superficial daily news and media accounts cannot compensate for in-depth diplomatic reports, richer in information, sources, analysis and recommendations (Vukadinoviæ, 1994: 248-249). Furthermore, others claim that the main functions of diplomacy have remained the same and that they represent one of the few stable foundations of international society. "It would not be surprising if this era was to be characterised not as the age of diplomacy's decline, but as the century of diplomacy" (Sofer, 1991: 78). Therefore, one calls also to the international public relations experts and practitioners, media consultants and spin-doctors working in the field of foreign policy alongside politicians and professional diplomats, not to merely apply different sophisticated techniques, but rather to strive to fill in "the ideological vacuum of the 3rd millennium."[8]

COMMUNICATIVE POTENTIAL OF SMALL DIPLOMACIES

No matter how convincing your strategic rationale for a given policy may be, it must, above all, be understood by a broader public, or else it may not be politically sustainable.[9]

This paper looked into the genesis of diplomacy as a concept, shifting in its meaning and function toward final destinations of a medialised reality and a pure communicative action. It showed that diplomacy became more or less media formatted and instrumented by communication, however, its basic content remains foreign policy as a way of how national interests of a particular country are formulated, implemented and co-ordinated in relation to other countries. Modern diplomats are locked in a specific relation of inter-dependency where they rely on media-transmitted information, on one side and on the other, use media as efficient communication means supplementing the classical diplomatic channels. Given such a situation, diplomatic profession nowadays resembles the profession of a public affairs practitioner, as it implements reasoning, tools and techniques of media and public relations. At this point it should be stressed again that in diplomacy, like in public relations, one should first and foremost be clear on what one wants to communicate, i.e., on the message, based on particular foreign affairs positions and shaped by public perceptions, at home and abroad.

Where does Slovenia stand in respect to the concepts and trends described in this paper? A small country, with limited resources and human capital, and with merely ten years of statehood, independent foreign policy and diplomatic experience, is probably not comparable to elaborated systems of (public) diplomacy in powerful Western countries like United States or Germany. Due to its size determinants, Slovenia's positioning in international affairs is specific, and also the potential ways in which its foreign policy can be efficiently implemented and communicated differ from the others.

As at the start, Slovenia was "a nation without an image and known identity" (Serajnik, 1998: 687); today it is widely recognised as a stable, prospective country in Central Europe, proved to be able to take on a role of "an exporter of stability" to the region, a mediator and "an honest broker" in international community. The pictures and the words of the former US President Clinton during his visit to Slovenia on 21 June 1999 bear historic importance of communicating Slovenia's role in the world: "We must build a Europe with no frontline states–a Europe undivided, democratic, and at peace for the first time in history. And Slovenia can lead the way."[10] One can claim that within the multilateral international organisations, Slovene diplomacy made an excellent use of its smallness and unproblematic position and can profit even more within the EU integration processes (Jazbec, 2001). The CFSP framework provides it, as an associated country, with an equal participation in the established co-ordination and communication practices which can contribute to rationalisations in the diplomatic apparatus. All in all, the very ability to communicate competently in the international affairs can importantly add up to the soft powers of Slovenia's cultural, civilisational and economic achievements, which exceed the physical power of the state.[11]

In order to compensate for its limited scope and power, Slovene diplomacy should work toward being more transparent, inclusive and communicative–it should build networks on all levels to include all relevant actors and provide for a synergy of diverse efforts in the field of public diplomacy and international public relations. Special attention should be devoted to media-related work: work of Slovene diplomats to a great extent relies on international media reporting, and the international media, in turn, can importantly strengthen Slovene foreign policy positions. Here, one observes that Slovene foreign policy actors tend to often use the domestic media as a communication channel and also, a testing variable, while Slovene media seem to be increasingly interested in performing as official representatives (and defenders) of Slovene national interests. Further more, communication and messages by Slovene diplomats and foreign policy actors should be based on thorough analysis and well-thought foreign policy formulations, on one side, and any foreign policy decision should take into account also public opinion and communication aspects. As there exists a stronger need for each and every single Slovene diplomat to integrate traditional diplomatic functions alongside the communication and media-related functions, it is very important to educate future professionals not only in international relations and foreign affairs, but also to train them in media and public relations.[12] At the same time one should provide that media and public relations practitioners get actively involved in foreign affairs and diplomatic activities, also by rotating in their job positions at the Foreign Ministry and the Slovene embassies abroad.

While attempting to position the Slovene diplomacy within the current trends of the international community and the communication society, one can only conclude that while these may be of advantage to the diplomacy of a small, but prospective country, its shortcomings in physical powers can be even better compensated by soft powers of communication. A Slovene diplomat, connected to the World Wide Web, providing a stronger bridge with media and the public, and being overall synergic and integrative in his/her communication function, can be even more efficient and effective in making the Slovene foreign policy voice heard, recognised and followed around the world.

NOTES

1. In Barston, 1988: 1. Thus, within its various definitions diplomacy can be understood as a formulation and implementation of a foreign policy; as a technique of a foreign policy; as international negotiations; and as an activity performed by diplomats. The common denominator of these definitions would be diplomacy defined as a primary method by means of which foreign policy is implemented and the usual means of communication in international affairs (Vukadinoviæ, 1994: 107-109). "Policy is formulation and direction; diplomacy is communication and implementation. It is the lubricant of the foreign policy machinery" (Olson, 1991: 60).

2. Some authors use Jürgen Habermas's theory of communicative action to describe the process of so called *diplomatic communicative interaction* in which cooperation is conceptualised as a social relationship conducted inside a complex web of intersubjective social structures of principles, norms, and rules produced and reproduced in the communicative interaction between states (Lose, 2001: 180). Diplomatic interaction is characterised by behaviour oriented towards mutual understanding, where perceptions of reality, interests, preferences, and desirable behaviour are subjected to a collective process of interpretation guided by argumentative rationality and the claim of validity. Collective understanding is constructed through diplomatic communicative interaction, i.e., on the basis of discussion, information gathering, and the desire to coordinate behaviour in order to minimize interstate friction (Lose, 2001: 188-190).

3. On additional requirements for a modern diplomat, see Macomber, 1991.

4. Howard Cincotta, USIA's Information Bureau, in State Magazine, February 1999. At *(www.state.gov/www/publications.statemag/statemag_feb99)*.

5. In fact, it is difficult to establish any direct relationships between public opinion, foreign policy and the conduct of diplomacy. Two contradictory lines of thought can be distinguished, the first arguing about the volatility and inadequacy of public opinion as a stable and effective foreing policy, whereas the second considers public attitudes quite stable and consistent over time and actually exercising a strong influence on foreign policy-making (Risse-Kappen, 1991). Some authors claim that within the context of open diplomacy the analysis of public opinion is usually one-sided, taking into account only the impact of something called "the populace" on the statesman, the diplomat or the military leader. "Public opinion, however, is not an autonomous force; it is frequently organised by voluntary organisations or a specific political group" (Sofer, 1991: 73). Therefore, one should analyse public opinion and foreign policy, as well as diplomacy, as in the process of interaction, constructing each other through existent domestic coalitions and policy networks (Plavšak, 1996a).

6. From a videoconference with Barry Fulton, Associate Director of USIA, and Tom Genton, Foreign Service Institute, US Embassy, Ljubljana, May 2001.

7. "Oesterreichs Diplomaten im 21. Jahrhundert," guest editorial by Ernst Sucharipa, Director of Diplomatic Academy in Vienna, Die Presse, 23 September 2000.

8. Interview with Paddy Ashdown, ex-leader of the British Liberals, Die Presse, 23 November 2000.

9. NATO Secretary General Lord Robertson in a speech "Communicate," Erasmus University, Rotterdam, 23 April 2001.

10. Remarks by President Clinton, Congress Square, Ljubljana, 21 June 1999. At *(http://clinton.hal.si/eng/clf01_3.html)*.

11. Dimitrij Rupel, Foreign Minister of Republic of Slovenia, at a lecture "Unions and Disunions," Faculty of Social Sciences, Ljubljana, 17 January 2001. At *(www.gov.si/mzz/eng/index.html)*.

12. A proposal by the Department of International Relations, Faculty of Social Sciences, University of Ljubljana, to the Slovene Foreign Ministry includes a workshop "Public Diplomacy and International Communications," to be on the curriculum of the Diplomatic Academy in the upcoming academic year.

BIBLIOGRAPHY

Alexandre, Laurien. (1987). In the service of the state: Public diplomacy, government media and Ronald Reagan. *Media, Culture and Society*, Vol. 9, 29-46.

Barston, R.P. (1988). *Modern Diplomacy*. London, New York: Longman.

Gergen, David R. (1991). Diplomacy in a Television Age. The Dangers of Teledemocracy. In Simon Sertafy (ed.), *The Media and Foreign Policy*. New York: St. Martin Press.

Grunig, James E. (1993). Public Relations and International Affairs. Effects, Ethics and Responsibility. *Journal of International Affairs*, 47 (1), 137-162.

Harnay, David. (2000). Europe's Common Foreign and Security Policy. Year 1. *European Foreign Affairs Review* 5, 275-280.

Heusgen, Christoph. (2000). The EU Foreign, Security and Defence Policy Planning and Early Warning Unit. *Challenge Europe–On-Line Journal of the European Policy Centre* (Brussels). At *(www.theepc.be/Challenge_Europe/text/memo.asp?ID=526)*.

Jazbec, Milan. (2001). *Diplomacies of new small states*. London: Ashgate.

Joergensen, Knud Erik. (1999). Modern European Diplomacy. A Research Agenda. *Journal of International Relations and Development*, Vol. 2 (1), 78-96.

Kevin, Deidre. (2001). Coverage of the European Parliament Elections of 1999. National Public Spheres and European Debates. *Javnost*, Vol. 8 (1), 21-38.

Kunczik, Michael. (1993). Public Relations fuer Staaten. Die Imagepflege von Nationen als Aspekt der internationalen Kommunikation: Zum Forschungsstand. 164-184.

Kunelius, Risto, and Sparks, Colin. (2001). Problems with a European Public Sphere. Introduction. *Javnost*, Vol. 8 (1), 5-20.

Lose, Lars G. (2001). Communicative Action and the World of Diplomacy. In Karin M. Fierke and Knud Erik Joergensen (ed.), *Constructing International Relations. The Next Generation*, 179-201. Armonk, New York: M. E. Sharpe.

Macomber, William B. (1991). First-Rate People, Third-Rate System. In William C. Olson (ed.), *The Theory and Practice of International Relations.* 78-83. New Jersey: Prentice Hall.

Manheim, Jarol B. and Albritton, Robert B. (1984). Changing National Images: International Public Relations and Media Agenda Setting. *The American Political Science Review,* Vol. 78, 641-657.

Monar, Joerg. (2000). The Case for a Diplomatic Academy of the European Union. *European Foreign Affairs Review* 5, 281-286.

Nicholson, Harold. (1988; 1939). *Diplomacy.* Washington: Institute for the Study of Diplomacy, Georgetown University.

Olson, William C. (1991; 1960). *The Theory and Practice of International Relations.* New Jersey: Prentice Hall.

Palmer, John. (2000). Europe in the World–Growing Up at Last. *Challenge Europe-On-Line Journal of the European Policy Centre* (Brussels). At *(www.theepc.be/Challenge_Europe/text/memo.asp?ID=277).*

Plavšak, Kristina. (1996a). *Why do small states want to join the European integration? Responses of Austria, Norway and Switzerland to the EC challenge.* Research paper, Columbia University-School of International and Public Affairs, New York.

Plavšak, Kristina. (1996b). *Implementation of Common Foreign and Securtiy Policy of the EU in the framework of the United Nations.Coordination of positions on the UN reform and its implications.* Research paper, Columbia University & Mission of the Republic of Slovenia to the United Nations, New York.

Plavšak, Kristina. (1994). Evropska identiteta v skupnem avdiovizualnem prostoru (European identity in the common audiovisual area). *Teorija in praksa,* vol.31 (7-8), 708-717.

Rangarajan, L.N. (1998). Diplomacy, States and Secrecy in Communications. *Diplomacy & Statecraft,* Vol. 9 (3), 18-49.

Risse-Kappen, Thomas. (1991). Public Opinion, Domestic Structures, and Foreign Policy in Liberal Democracies. *World Politics,* Vol. 43, 479-512.

Rothkopf, David J. (1998). Cyberpolitik: The Changing Nature of Power in the Information Age. *Journal of International Affairs,* Vol. 51 (2), 325-359.

Serajnik Sraka, Nada. (1998). Kako komunicira dr_ava z mednarodnimi javnostmi: Primer Slovenije (How a state communicates with the international publics: Case of Slovenia). *Teorija in praksa,* 35 (4), 686-701.

Shea, Jamie. (1999). *The Kosovo Crisis and the Media. Reflections of a NATO Spokesman,* Address to the Summer Forum on Kosovo organised by the Atlantic Council of the UK and the Trades Union Committee for European and Transatlantic Understanding. Reform Club, London, 15. July 1999.

Signitzer, Benno H. and Coombs, Timothy. (1992). Public Relations and Public Diplomacy. Conceptual Convergences. *Public Relations Review,* 18 (2), 137-147.

Sofer, Sasson. (1991). Debate Revisited: Practice over Theory? In William C. Olson (ed.), *The Theory and Practice of International Relations,* 65-78. New Jersey: Prentice Hall.

Solana, Javier. (2000). Developments in CFSP over the past year. *Challenge Europe–On-Line Journal of the European Policy Centre* (Brussels). At *(www.theepc.be/Challenge_Europe/text/memo.asp?ID=180).*

Stephanopoulos, George. (1999). *All Too Human. A Political Education*. Boston, New York, London: Little, Brown and Company.

Thussu Kissan, Daya. (2000). Media Wars and Public Diplomacy. *Javnost/The Public*, Vol.7 (3), 5-18.

Vukadinoviæ, Radovan. (1994). *Diplomacija. Strategija politiènih pogajanj. (Diplomacy. The Strategy of Political Negotiations)*. Ljubljana: Arah Consulting.

Wilcox, Dennis L., Ault, Philip H. and Agee, Warren K. (1998). *Public Relations Strategies and Tactics*, Fifth Edition, Addison Wesley Longman, Inc.

Models of Voter Behavior:
The 2000 Slovenia Parliamentary Elections

Dejan Verčič
Iztok Verdnik

Pristop Communications, Slovenia

SUMMARY. This article reports on a test of a predictive model of voter behavior in Slovenia. The study is based on Slovenian parliamentary elections held on 15 October 2000. A survey was made in an electoral unit ("Vrhnika"). This is one of the tests that were simultaneously done in three countries–Poland, the US and Slovenia. The purpose of the test reported in this study was to test the model in a different cultural and political setting from the one in which it was designed, and also in a different electoral setting–in a proportional instead of majority system of voting. The model proved itself as working in Slovenia. *[Article copies available for a fee from The Haworth Document Delivery Service: 1-800-HAWORTH. E-mail address: <getinfo@haworthpressinc.com> Website: <http://www.HaworthPress.com> © 2002 by The Haworth Press, Inc. All rights reserved.]*

KEYWORDS. Elections, Slovenia, political candidates, political parties, voter behavior

---

Dejan Verčič and Iztok Verdnik are affiliated with Pristop Communications, Trubarjeva c. 79, 1000 Ljubljana, Slovenia (E-mail: dejan.vercic@pristop.si or E-mail: iztok.verdnik@pristop.si).

[Haworth co-indexing entry note]: "Models of Voter Behavior: The 2000 Slovenia Parliamentary Elections." Verčič, Dejan, and Iztok Verdnik. Co-published simultaneously in *Journal of Political Marketing* (The Haworth Political Press, an imprint of The Haworth Press, Inc.) Vol. 1, No. 2/3, 2002, pp. 123-135; and: *Communication of Politics: Cross-Cultural Theory Building in the Practice of Public Relations and Political Marketing* (eds: Bruce I. Newman, and Dejan Verčič) The Haworth Political Press, an imprint of The Haworth Press, Inc., 2002, pp. 123-135. Single or multiple copies of this article are available for a fee from The Haworth Document Delivery Service [1-800-HAWORTH, 9:00 a.m. - 5:00 p.m. (EST). E-mail address: getinfo@haworthpressinc.com].

10.1300/J199v01n02_09 *123*

INTRODUCTION

This study reports on one of the three applications of a predictive model of voter behavior executed in a cross-cultural study in 2000. The first was carried out on the presidential elections in Poland (Falkowski and Cwalina, 2001), the second in the USA (Newman, 2001) and this, the third one, on the parliamentary elections in Slovenia. The model in this study was operationalized at both the candidate and party level (as it was in the USA; see Newman, 2001). The study sought to identify those questions that were unique to both candidates and political parties that drove behavior of the voters in this election.

While Newman's (2001) study in the USA indicated that the used model of voter behavior works equally well on candidate as on the party level, this was impossible to test in Slovenia. Similarly to Odescalchi's (1999) experience in Hungary, we found such a low visibility (Rein, Kotler and Stoller, 1997) of candidates among their potential voters that it was impossible to measure data with any accuracy separately for candidates and parties. Since voters were generally capable of identifying parties only, we tested the model on the party level.

A MODEL OF VOTER BEHAVIOR
IN EVOLVING DEMOCRACY

A model of voter behavior was developed and tested by Newman in the USA. "The fundamental axiom of the model is that voters are consumers of service offered by a politician, and similar to consumers on the commercial marketplace, voters choose candidates based on the perceived value offered to them. The model proposes that there are five distinct and separate cognitive domains that drive voters' behavior" (Newman 1999b: 260): political issues, social imagery, candidate personality, situational contingency, and epistemic value (for review of the model and some of its tests see Newman, 1999b; Newman and Sheth, 1985; Newman and Sheth, 1987; also Newman, 2001; Falkowski and Cwalina, 2001; Verčič, 1999).

It can be claimed that nowhere are politicians "in the business of selling hope to people" (Newman, 1999a: 7) more than in evolving democracies. "Obviously, the collapse of the communist ideology has eliminated communism as a political governance option. The only acceptable alternatives are political anarchy and the threat of civil wars or the embracement of a democratic form of government. Since political anarchy is not in the self-interest of the politicians, it is more likely that a market-oriented approach to getting elected and reelected will be embraced in most emerging democracies" (Sheth, 1994: ix).

It looks like contemporary emergence of democracy is corresponding to emergence of political marketing: in emerging democracies it is not a candidate that behaves as "service provider" (Newman, 1994: 9), but his political party (cf. Odescalchi, 1999). This is even more so in countries, like Slovenia, with proportional electoral systems.

A primer gives the following description of Slovenian electoral system:

> The Slovenian electoral system is essentially proportional–meaning that each party get a number of deputies equal to the share of votes they received at the polls–but it also has elements of a majority system. Namely, voters are divided into 88 electoral districts and voters within each district vote for individual candidates. Electoral districts are integrated into eight electoral units. The personalization of candidates is guaranteed by the fact that candidate lists are comprised of those candidates who received the highest share of votes in the electoral units in which they ran. Because of this, candidates within the same party also compete against each other which creates a great deal of uncertainty in elections. According to this system, which remained valid until 2000–parties could participate in dividing the remainder of votes if they obtained at least three deputies, i.e., more than 3.3% of votes. Parties were also allowed to form a national list creating an advantage for certain candidates.

> In 2000, a new constitutional law introduced a 4% electoral threshold for entry into the National Assembly and that "the lists of candidates who received less than 4% of votes will not be taken unto account. Instead, the Droop quotient will be used in allotting mandates per electoral units. In addition, the law determined that assigning mandates to party lists on the state level should equal those which would have been assigned based on the sum total of votes in all the electoral units. The last provision means that beside direct mandates, which lists can get in an electoral unit for every 8.33% votes, additional mandates that account for the difference to the actually reached percentage of the votes on the state level belong to lists, too. According to the new law, there are no additional direct mandates if a party list does not receive more than 4% of the vote on the state level. This new regulation enables each electoral unit to have 11 electoral deputies; this regulation did not apply in the previous system because of the national lists." (Lukšič 2001: 41-42)

If the above explanation looks complicated, it is only because the electoral system is complicated. It is, therefore, easy to understand why voters don't care to learn about the individual candidates and focus their attention on parties instead.

OVERVIEW OF THE STUDY

Setting

The 2000 parliamentary elections were the third elections after the adoption of the Constitutional Charter on the Sovereignty and Independence of the Republic of Slovenia in 1991, when Slovenia transformed itself from a Yugoslav, socialist federal republic into an independent, open and democratic country. Slovenian parliament consists of 90 members. The country is divided into 8 electoral units and each of these consists of 11 electoral districts. (Two seats are reserved for members of constitutionally recognized national minorities in Slovenia, Hungarians and Italians, who vote separately.)

The election date was October 15, 2000. Electoral body consisted of 1.5 million voters. Participation on parliamentary elections was around 70 percent.

The study was carried out approximately 2 weeks before parliamentary elections in electoral district Vrhnika, a suburban area near Ljubljana, the capital of Slovenia. This district was selected based on similarity of its electoral result (on the party level) to previous (1996) parliamentary elections. Based on pre-election polls by several research institutions, three political parties predicted to win the most votes were selected for study. They were LDS (Liberal Democrats of Slovenia), ZLSD (United List of Social Democrats), and SDS (Social Democrats of Slovenia).

Respondents were interviewed via telephone. Interviewing started two weeks before elections and was completed in four days. The Computer Assisted Telephone Interviewing (CATI) was used to obtain respondents' intentions regarding voting. One day after elections a post-election contact was made with the respondents of the study to obtain information on the electoral decision of the respondents a day earlier.

Sample

The study was to be carried on samples of 200 voters per each selected political party (see Table 1). Random sampling was based on households and of respondents within them. Four thousand, five hundred, sixty-four contacts and 617 interviews were made in accordance with the sampling procedures before elections.

The day after elections 87.5 percent of the original sample (N = 617) was interviewed to obtain data on the actual voting decision.

Questionnaire Design

The questionnaire included statements that were operationalized along the lines of the components of the model of voter behavior. A total of 230 questions were included in the survey. Of the total number of questions, approximately one-half dealt with the candidates and one-half dealt with the parties.

Data Analysis

Following Newman's (cf. 2001) suggestion, the principal technique used in data analysis was discriminant analysis. Three sets of pairwise discriminant analyses were carried out between correspondents who indicated that they preferred each party (LDS, ZLSD and SDS). In these analyses, the criterion variable was the respondent's preferred political party. The predictor variables were questions generated for each of the components in the theory using a series of pairwise T-tests between respondent groups (LDS versus ZLSD, LDS versus SDS and ZLSD versus SDS).

DISCUSSION

LDS vs. ZLSD

The data results in Table 2 report on the discriminant analysis carried out between respondents who said that they will vote either LDS or ZLSD. Specifically, the respondents indicated likelihood that they would vote for each of these parties in the upcoming parliamentary elections. The four most important values to voters who identified themselves as LDS supporters were, in order of importance:

1. Future-orientation;
2. Support for the poorest;
3. Higher salaries; and
4. Quality education.

TABLE 1. General Profile of Sample

Study Timing	Approx. 10 Days Before General Elections	
Sample Size	617 Cases, at Least 200 for Each Candidate	
Method	CATI	
Age of Sample		
	18-30 y.	20.1%
	31-54 y.	42.8%
	55 and More	37.1%
Education of Sample		
	Primary School or Less	12.0%
	Trade School	8.8%
	Secondary School	55.9%
	2 Years of University	11.8%
	University Level or More	11.3%
	Missing	.2%
Social Class of Sample		
	Lower Class	4.5%
	Lower Middle	18.2%
	Middle	61.9%
	Upper Middle	13.0%
	Upper	1.1%
	Missing	1.3%
Questionnaire	Approx. 230 Questions; 2 Levels (Party and Candidate Level)	
Party Preference		
Will Vote	LDS	33.5 %
	SDS	31.4 %
	ZLSD	31.9 %
	Missing	3.1 %
Did Vote (Collected After the Elections)	LDS	33.2 %
	SDS	18.0 %
	ZLSD	22.5 %
	Missing	26.3 %
Party Loyalty		
	1.0 % of LDS Voters Are Also Members of the Party	
	6.3% of SDS Voters Are Also Members of the Party	
	7.9 % of ZLSD Voters Are Also Members of the Party	
Level of Interest/Concern in Election	20.4 % of Total Sample Very Concerned About Elections	

TABLE 2. Discriminant Analysis Results for Party Supporters, LDS vs. ZLSD–
Four Most Important Variables Listed for Each Party

A. LDS

I believe that my party is future-oriented.	.898
I believe that my party will make living easier for the poorest.	.776
I believe that my party will raise salaries.	.521
I believe that my party will assure quality of the education system.	.518

B. ZLSD

I believe that my party will assure equality of women's rights.	−.672
I would switch my vote if taxes rose.	−.618
I would switch my vote if my party's leaders were caught drinking while driving.	−.524
I would switch my vote if my party's leaders evaded taxes.	−.488

Eigenvalue	1.898
Wilks' Lambda	.345
Chi-Squared	85.127
df	64
Significance	.040

Classification Results

			Predicted Group Membership		
			1.00	2.00	Total
Original	Count	LDS	59	8	67
		ZLSD	3	44	47
	%	LDS	88.1	11.9	100.0
		ZLSD	6.4	93.6	100.0

Correctly classified:	90.4 %

A review of the top four issues shows why LDS is capable of being a party of a relative majority in the parliament throughout the first decade of democracy in Slovenia and why it was the pivotal player in nearly all governments in that period: because voters perceive it as being capable of thinking and bringing about future. At the same time it is perceived as being compassionate, considerate of government and public services employees and investing in educational system. It is no wonder that with such a profile, the party won these elections.

The four most important values to voters who identified themselves as ZLSD supporters were, in order of importance:

1. Women's rights;
2. Situational contingency–switch if taxes rose;
3. Situational contingency–switch if party's leaders were caught drinking while driving; and
4. Situational contingency–switch if party's leaders evaded taxes.

These four values show a high level of situational contingency involved in voter behavior in Slovenia. This can partly be explained by a lack of profound political choices European emerging democracies face which forces all political parties that compete for the central stage to support the same policies: liberalization and privatization (domestic policies), and EU and NATO membership (foreign policies). The discriminant model predicted respondents' voter behavior with 90.4% level of accuracy, which is less than found in Newman's (cf. 2001) study in the US, but still very good.

LDS vs. SDS

The data results in Table 3 report on the discriminant analysis carried out between voters who predicted that they will vote either LDS or SDS. Specifically, the respondents indicated likelihood that they would vote for each of these parties in the upcoming parliamentary elections. The four most important values to voters who identified themselves as LDS supporters were, in order of importance:

1. Situational contingency–switch if inflation rose significantly;
2. Situational contingency–switch if party's leaders were involved in an economic/business scandal;
3. Vote for my party because of the personalities that endorse it; and
4. The party will lower crime rate.

An examination of these data shows that in the selected choice between LDS and SDS, LDS supporters choose it over SDS because of its leaders on the national level. This result also confirms that voters in the selected electoral district were voting based on national party preferences and not for their local candidates. It looks like these voters were

TABLE 3. Discriminant Analysis Results for Party Supporters, LDS vs. SDS–
Four Most Important Variables Listed for Each Party

A. LDS

I would switch my vote if inflation rose significantly.	−.692
I would switch my vote if my party's leaders were involved in an economic/business scandal.	−.459
I am voting for my party because of the personalities that endorse it.	−.447
I believe that my party will lower crime rate.	−.400

B. SDS

Blue-collar workers will most likely vote for my party.	.400
I believe my party will start worrying less about the world problems and more about our domestic problems.	.382
I will vote for my party because I want a change in the administration.	.350
Farmers will most likely vote for my party.	.333

Eigenvalue	1.177
Wilks' Lambda	.459
Chi-Squared	96.845
df	63
Significance	.004

Classification Results

			Predicted Group Membership		
			LDS	SDS	Total
Original	Count	LDS	56	11	67
		SDS	12	79	91
	%	LDS	83.6	16.4	100.0
		SDS	13.2	86.8	100.0
Correctly classified:					85.4 %

satisfied with the way LDS was running economy and would switch if
inflation significantly rose (a demon from Yugoslav past, when people
learned how to live with inflation above 1,000 percent).

The four most important values to voters who identified themselves
as SDS supporters were, in order of importance:

1. Blue collar worker's support;
2. The party will stop worrying about the world problems and start worrying about domestic problems;
3. I want change in the administration; and
4. Farmers' support.

These values confirm positioning of SDS as the main opposition to LDS. Its supporters are from lower social strata and non-urban areas, parochial and demanding more radical changes in the evolution of new Slovenia. The discriminant model predicted respondents' voter behavior with 85.4% level of accuracy.

ZLSD vs. SDS

The data results in Table 4 report on the discriminant analysis carried out between potential voters of ZLSD or SDS. Specifically, the respondents indicated likelihood that they would vote for each of these parties in the upcoming parliamentary elections. The four most important values to voters who identified themselves as ZLSD supporters were, in order of importance:

1. The party will offer job security;
2. I believe the party is sincere;
3. Situational contingency–switch if economic results aggravated; and
4. Vote for the party because of the personalities that endorse it.

Of all the parties in Slovenia, ZLSD is generally perceived as being representing continuity and moderation in its support to social, economic and political transformations. Little change to many people means little insecurity. This would change only if economic results aggravated. Also, this result confirms that voters in the selected electoral district were voting based on national party preferences and not for their local candidates.

The four most important values to voters who identified themselves as SDS supporters were, in order of importance:

1. I believe that the party will raise salaries;
2. Foreign born voters will most likely vote for this party;
3. Situational contingency–switch if party's leaders were not healthy enough to go through their mandate; and
4. Situational contingency–switch if inflation rose significantly.

TABLE 4. Discriminant Analysis Results for Party Supporters, ZLSD vs. SDS–
Four Most Important Variables Listed for Each Party

A. ZLSD

I believe my party will offer me job security.	−.656
I believe my party is sincere.	−.497
I would switch my vote if economic results aggravated.	−.413
I am voting for my party because of the personalities that endorse it.	−.400

B. SDS

I believe my party will raise salaries.	.605
Foreign born voters will most likely vote for my party.	.549
My party's leaders were not healthy enough to go through their mandate.	.490
I would switch my vote if inflation rose significantly.	.488

Eigenvalue	1.113
Wilks' Lambda	.473
Chi-Squared	77.797
df	64
Significance	.115

Classification Results

			Predicted Group Membership		Total
			SDS	ZLSD	
Original	Count	SDS	81	10	91
		ZLSD	7	40	47
	%	SDS	89.0	11.0	100.0
		ZLSD	14.9	85.1	100.0
Correctly classified:					87.7%

Foreign-born voters in this context means descendants of political emigration that was forced to leave Slovenia when communists were in power. The support of descendants of Slovenian political Diaspora for SDS was communicated well and the potential voters noticed that. In this pair between the two social-democratic parties (which ZLSD and

SDS are–at least by their names) it is interesting to note what their potential voters expect from them in labor-related terms. As seen above, ZLSD supporters expect job security (which confirms that ZLSD is more middle class social democratic party), while SDS supporters would like to get higher salaries (with SDS being more blue collar social democratic party). The discriminant model predicted respondents' voter behavior with 87.7% level of accuracy.

CONCLUSION

This study reported on a test of a predictive model of voter behavior in Slovenia. This is one of the tests that were simultaneously done in three countries–Poland, the US and Slovenia. The purpose of the test reported in this study was to test the model in a different cultural and political setting from the one in which it was designed, and also in a different electoral setting–in a proportional instead of majority system of voting.

The model proved itself as working in Slovenia. Its classification results, reported in Tables 2, 3 and 4 are not as high as originally reported by Newman, but they are nevertheless high enough to make a predictive model of voter behavior viable also beyond the nation boundaries of its conception.

The 2000 parliamentary elections viewed through the glasses of the model used here show that voters selected LDS for its future orientation, ZLSD for stability and SDS for change. This makes the top three choices of Slovenian electorate a balanced selection that proves that democracy gained its ground in Slovenia the past decade. The balance between stability and change with a view to the future is an indication that democracy in Slovenia is transforming itself from evolving into evolved.

Although it was not in the focus of this study, similarly to Odescalchi's experience in Hungary we found low visibility of individual local candidates in parliamentary elections is Slovenia. Although this may be partly explained by a proportional electoral system, it also demonstrates low effort on the side of individual politicians–first as candidates, but maybe even later, if elected, as officials. The further adoption of political marketing models and methods in evolving democracies may well be linked to the question of individual responsibility of politicians.

REFERENCES

Falkowski, Andrzej, and Wojciech Cwalina. "Structural Models of Voter Behavior in Polish Presidential Election 2000." Paper presented to the 8th International Public Relations Research Symposium. Bled, Slovenia, 2001.

Lukšič, Igor. *The Political System of the Republic of Slovenia: A Primer.* Transl. Erica Johnson Debeljak. Ljubljana: Znanstveno in publicistièno središèe, 2001.

Newman, Bruce I. *The Marketing of the President: Political Marketing as Campaign Strategy.* Thousand Oaks, CA: Sage, 1994.

Newman, Bruce I. "Politics in an Age of Manufactured Images." *Journal for Mental Changes*, 5, No. 2, 1999a, pp. 7-25.

Newman, Bruce I. "A Predictive Model of Voter Behavior: The Repositioning of Bill Clinton." In B. I. Newman (ed.), *Handbook of Political Marketing*, Thousand Oaks, CA: Sage, 1999b, pp. 259-282.

Newman, Bruce I. "Models of Voter Behavior in Traditional and Evolving Democracies: The 2000 U.S. Presidential Election." Paper presented to the 8th International Public Relations Research Symposium, Bled, Slovenia, 2001.

Newman, Bruce I., and Jagdish N. Sheth. *A Theory of Political Choice Behavior.* New York: Praeger, 1987.

Newman, Bruce I., and Jagdish N. Sheth. "Model of Primary Voter Behavior." *Journal of Consumer Research*, 12, No. 2, pp. 178-187.

Odescalchi, Daniel. "Democracy and Elections in the New East Central Europe." In B. I. Newman (ed.), *Handbook of Political Marketing*, Thousand Oaks, CA: Sage, 1999, pp. 587-603.

Rein, Irving, Philip Kotler and Martin Stoller. *High Visibility: The Making and Marketing of Professionals into Celebrities.* Lincolnwood (Chicago), IL: NTC Business Books, 1997.

Sheth, Jagdish N. "Foreword." In B. I. Newman, *The Marketing of the President: Political Marketing as Campaign Strategy.* Thousand Oaks, CA: Sage, 1994, pp. ix-xi.

Verčič, Dejan. "The Politics of Total Communication." *Journal for Mental Changes*, 5, No. 2, 1999, pp. 51-64.

Structural Models of Voter Behavior in the 2000 Polish Presidential Election

Andrzej Falkowski
Wojciech Cwalina

*Warsaw School of Advanced Social Psychology
and Catholic University of Lublin*

SUMMARY. The data of the 2000 Polish presidential election have been analyzed according to Newman and Sheth's model of voter's choice behavior (1985). Although this model was originally interpreted within the statistical perspective of discriminant analysis, it could be also extended within the framework of structural equation methodology. Namely, if the seven cognitive domains (Issues and Policies, Emotional Feelings, Candidate Image, Current Events, Epistemic Issues, Social Imagery and Epistemic Issues) are assumed to be distinct and separate, they can be treated as independent (predictive) variables with the voter's intention as a dependent or predicted variable. The three models were

---

Andrzej Falkowski and Wojciech Cwalina are affiliated with the Warsaw School of Advanced Social Psychology and Catholic University of Lublin.

Address correspondence to: Andrzej Falkowski or Wojciech Cwalina, Department of Psychology, Warsaw School of Advanced Social Psychology, ul. Chodakowska 19/31, 03-815 Warsaw, Poland (E-mail: andyfalk@sunlib.p.lodz.pl or wojciech.cwalina@swps. edu.pl).

This paper is an extended version of the authors' presentation at the International Public Relations Research Symposium: *Politics of Communication and Communication of Politics*. Slovenia: Bled, 6-8 July 2001.

[Haworth co-indexing entry note]: "Structural Models of Voter Behavior in the 2000 Polish Presidential Election." Falkowski, Andrzej, and Wojciech Cwalina. Co-published simultaneously in *Journal of Political Marketing* (The Haworth Political Press, an imprint of The Haworth Press, Inc.) Vol. 1, No. 2/3, 2002, pp. 137-158; and: *Communication of Politics: Cross-Cultural Theory Building in the Practice of Public Relations and Political Marketing* (eds: Bruce I. Newman, and Dejan Verčič) The Haworth Political Press, an imprint of The Haworth Press, Inc., 2002, pp. 137-158. Single or multiple copies of this article are available for a fee from The Haworth Document Delivery Service [1-800-HAWORTH, 9:00 a.m. - 5:00 p.m. (EST). E-mail address: getinfo@haworthpressinc.com].

tested and the results of path analysis show the complex pattern of mutual interdependence between the cognitive domains and voter behavior. The specificity of the cause-effect relationship obtained by the structural equation methodology presented in the paper allows us to put forward some practical suggestions regarding the way electoral campaigns should be conducted. *[Article copies available for a fee from The Haworth Document Delivery Service: 1-800-HAWORTH. E-mail address: <getinfo@ haworthpressinc.com> Website: <http://www.HaworthPress.com> © 2002 by The Haworth Press, Inc. All rights reserved.]*

KEYWORDS. Presidential election, media, voter behavior, structural equation modeling, emotional feelings, advertisements

Together with the development of the system of democracy around the world, there has grown an increased interest on the part of scientists as well as political marketing specialists in the factors and rules underlying citizens' voting behavior. Since the 1940s researchers have been putting forward voting behavior models with increasing predictive power. We can distinguish three main paradigms of voter behavior analysis: sociological (Berelson, Lazarsfeld & McPhee, 1954; Lazarsfeld, Berelson & Gaudet, 1948), socio-psychological (Campbell, Converse, Miller & Stokes, 1960; Converse, 1964) and economic (Downs, 1957; Popkin, 1991). Together with the development of research methodology and the emergence of new theories, these paradigms have been constantly evolving, and a number of changes and supplements have been introduced. However, the changes in societies' political culture and life indicate that these three, often complementary, research perspectives, are not sufficient to effectively predict voter behavior (see Dalton & Wattenberg, 1993; Page, 1977; Riley, 1988).

Another, more advanced step in the development of voter behavior analysis are multivariate models, which are created across the "old" paradigms (Johnston, Pattie & Allsopp, 1988; Newman & Sheth, 1985; Singh, Leong, Tan & Wang, 1995). These models have been subject to empirical tests during elections at various levels and in different countries and seem to offer a better chance to explain the foundations of voter behavior. They are also an important source of information for practitioners of political marketing. They allow them to base marketing decisions on a more solid scientific basis by providing them with knowledge as to what data might be needed to better plan a campaign and to better use funds to achieve success.

One proposal that offers promising theoretical and applicational solutions is Newman and Sheth's voter's choice behavior model (1985; see also Newman, 1999; Verčič, 1999). According to this model the following seven domains are assumed to guide voter behavior: (1) *Issues and Policies*–refers to a list of salient issues and policies, including economics, foreign, social policies as well as leadership characteristics; (2) *Social Imagery*–refers to all relevant segments of the voting population likely to be supportive of the candidates being studied; (3) *Emotional Feelings*–represent the voters' emotional attitude toward the candidates; (4) *Candidate Image*–refers to the candidate's image based on personality traits; (5) *Current Events*–refers to issues and policies which develop during the course of the campaign; (6) *Personal Events*– refers to situations in the personal life of the candidate; and (7) *Epistemic Issues*–refers to those aspects of the candidate that would provide the perceived satisfaction of voters' curiosity, knowledge, and exploratory needs. These cognitive domains are presented in Figure 1.

Although the model as simplified by Newman (1999), using only five domains (Political Issues, Social Imagery, Candidate Personality, Situational Contingency and Epistemic Value), was employed in testing the voter behavior during the 1996 US presidential election, the present theoretical and empirical analyses use the broader approach, including all seven domains of original research by Newman and Sheth (1985).

FIGURE 1. Model of Voter's Choice Behavior (Newman & Sheth, 1985: 179)

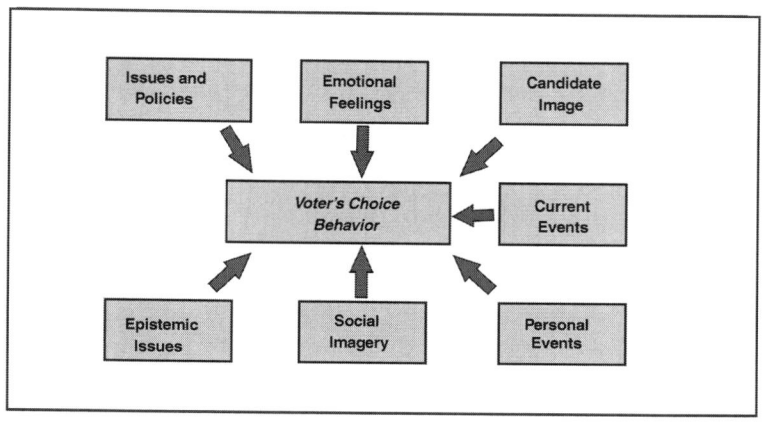

If the seven cognitive domains are assumed to be distinct and separate, then they can be incorporated into the discriminant analysis as independent (predictive) variables, with voting intention being a dependent or predicted variable. However, the question arises whether the domains are, in fact, distinct and separate. For example, it is well documented in psychological literature that cognitive and emotional elements should be treated not as separate, but as interactive vectors (e.g., Cwalina & Falkowski, 2000; Falkowski & Cwalina, 1999; Singh et al., 1995). Therefore, one can pose a question regarding possible causal relationships among the set of variables previously treated as distinct and independent. Replacing the traditional discriminant models with structural ones that could specify the interrelations among different cognitive domains can provide the answers to such questions (about structural equation analysis, see Loehlin, 1987).

Asking which element acts on another element is a problem of causal relationship among elements previously assumed to be distinct and independent variables. This concerns, in particular, the proper placement in this causal chain of a voter's emotional attitudes toward candidates.

Many studies have revealed that one's emotional attitude toward the candidates or political parties is a very good predictor of a voter's decision (e.g., Abelson, Kinder, Peters & Fiske, 1982; Masterson & Biggers, 1986). For instance, Lott, Lott and Saris (1993) found that in the 1988 US presidential campaign, a voter's preference correlated with his or her feelings toward the candidate on the level of $r = 0.68$ for Bush and $r = 0.60$ for Dukakis. Singh and his collaborators (1995), analyzing voters' attitudes just before the parliamentary elections in Singapore in 1988, by comparing multiple regressions, obtained a prediction of voters' intention on the basis of feelings toward the party and its candidates on the level of $R^2 = 0.36$ ($p < .0001$).

The relationship between emotion toward a candidate and intention to vote for him was also empirically verified during the Polish presidential election in 1995, when Lech Walesa (the incumbent) and Aleksander Kwasniewski (the challenger) were the two main competitors (Cwalina & Falkowski, 1999; Cwalina, Falkowski & Kaid, 2000; Falkowski & Cwalina, 1999). In order to verify whether general emotional attitude toward a candidate is a good predictor of voting intentions, a discriminant analysis was conducted. Table 1 shows the results we obtained, including the percentages of the participants correctly classified as Walesa's and Kwasniewski's electorates based on the feeling thermometer. The support for the candidate predicted on this basis was very

TABLE 1. Number and Percentage of the Subjects Attributed to Particular Electorates Based on the General Emotional Attitude Toward the Candidates: Results of the Discriminant Analysis (Falkowski & Cwalina, 1999: 290)

Observed voting intention	Predicted voting intention based on the thermometer of feelings					
	Aleksander Kwasniewski		Lech Walesa		Total	
	n	%	n	%	N	%
Aleksander Kwasniewski	91	**94.8**	5	5.2	96	100
Lech Walesa	5	6.1	77	**93.9**	82	100
Not declared	6	24.0	19	76.0	25	100

Eigenvalue = 2.729; Wilks λ = .268; χ^2 = 230.33; df = 2; p < 0.001

good: 94% of subjects was attributed correctly (95% for Kwasniewski's electorate and 94% for Walesa's electorate).

Additionally, the coefficient of point-biserial correlation between the emotional attitude toward the candidates and voting intention was very high (r_{pbi} = 0.845, p < 0.001).

The results pointing to the power of the relationship between emotions and decisions led Aronson, Wilson and Akert (1994) to suggest that people vote with their hearts rather than with their minds.

Before we can propose a reconstruction of Newman and Sheth's model of voter's choice behavior using structural equation methodology, it is necessary to consider the theoretical consequences of various causal dependencies between the variables mentioned in this model, with particular emphasis on the relationship between the emotional domain and the other six cognitive domains.

STRUCTURAL MODELS OF VOTER BEHAVIOR

The re-interpretation of Newman and Sheth's voter's choice behavior model needs, besides an attempt to determine causal relations between particular domains, to be completed by another factor–the media, especially the electronic media. Even though early research on the role of mass media in forming voting preferences pointed to their marginal importance (Lazarsfeld et al., 1948), currently it is generally assumed that the media form, to a large extent, both voter beliefs and voter feelings toward candidates for various political offices (e.g.,

Ansolabehere, Iyengar & Simon, 1995; Harrison, 1965; Kaid, 1999; Negrine, 1994).

One attempt at a precise specification of the media's influence is Falkowski and Cwalina's sequential model of advertising's influence on voting behavior (1999).

Sequential Model of Advertising Influence on Voting Behavior

The hypothetical dynamic process of advertising's impact on voting behavior is presented in Figure 2. The arrows indicate the causal relationship between the components. The model assumes that in order to recognize whether the spots change voters' decisions, it is necessary to find a link between the following four components: (1) cognitive/affective elements (image); (2) general feelings toward the candidate; (3) intention for whom to vote; and (4) decision for whom to vote.

The results of the empirical testing of the sequential model of advertising's influence on voting behavior during the parliamentary elections in Germany in 1994 and presidential elections in France and Poland in 1995 demonstrated, that political advertising can influence voting decisions in three ways (Cwalina, Falkowski & Kaid, 2000). First, advertisements could strengthen the already existing voting preferences. The supporters of a given candidate confirm their support for their candidate, whereas the opponents confirm their place in the opposition. In

FIGURE 2. Sequential Model of Advertising Influence on Voting Behavior (Falkowski & Cwalina, 1999: 228)

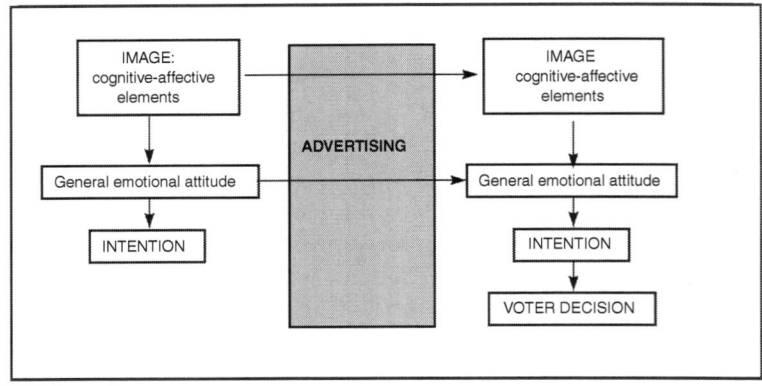

other words, the polarization of voting preferences increases. This can also be connected with a certain reconfiguration of the candidate's image in the minds of his electorate.

Second, advertisements could weaken already existing voting preferences and, in extreme cases, may even cause a change. This influence leads to an increase in uncertainty among voters about whom to support. It is usually accompanied by a reconfiguration of the candidate's image.

Third, advertisements could neither weaken nor strengthen political preferences, but they lead to the reconfiguration of the candidate's image in voters' minds. This type of influence can be called cognitive influence because, as a result of it, the argumentation of a previously-formed decision does change, but the direction and certainty with which it was made do not change.

Finally, no situation was found where advertising had no influence at all on voters. If the media and advertisements placed there always have an influence on voters, then it is fully justifiable to complete Newman and Sheth's with a media component.

Causal Models of Voting Behavior: A Reinterpretation of Newman and Sheth's Approach

The term "media" is understood here as an additional cognitive domain in terms of Newman and Sheth's model. That is, it reflects voters' beliefs or imaginations concerning the importance of media for political elections in general and voters' feelings of media influence on decision-making.

Reconfiguration of Newman and Sheth's model into structural equation methodology requires clarification of some causal effects. We will start from a simple structural model presented in Figure 3, which intuitively describes the dynamic process of voter behavior, and can be treated as the first hypotheses to be empirically tested.

Structural Equation Model I

Figure 3 shows that it is intuitively obvious that the six cognitive domains about the candidate are shaped by the media. That is, the media are the cause, and each of the cognitive domains is the effect. The group of paths connecting the elements in question represents this assumption.

The next group of paths in this complex causal relationship connects the cognitive domains with emotional feelings. In Newman and Sheth's

FIGURE 3. Structural Model of Voter Behavior I

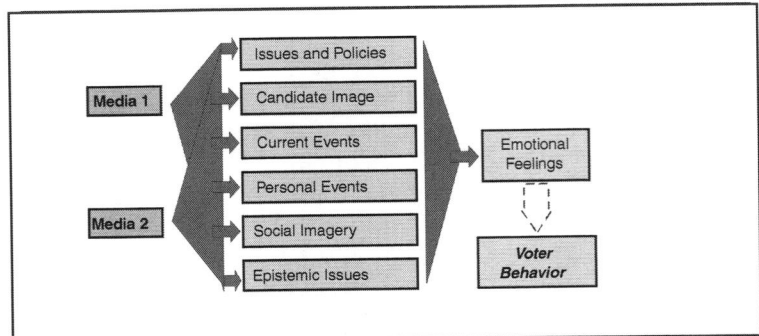

model this element stands for a separate domain as one of the independent elements that influences a voter's choice. However, based on the results of the research on the relationship between emotions and voting intention presented above, we assume that emotional feelings are a good predictor of voting intentions, i.e., the voter will choose the candidate who is "warmer," and evokes more positive emotions.

Structural Equation Model II

It is easy to see that one can assume some different combinations of the structural model presented in Figure 4. It is quite reasonable to assume that the media also influence the voter's emotional feelings. Therefore, besides the paths from media to cognitive domains we can add an additional path that directly connects the media with the emotional feelings. This second hypothesis is presented in Figure 4.

Structural Equation Model III

It may also be assumed that there exists a mutual interaction between the media and cognitive domains. That is, media influence the cognitive domains, as well as cognitive domains influence the media.

The assumptions concerning the role of the media in forming voting preferences or even the political scene are corroborated by various studies (e.g., Ansolabehere et al., 1995; Chaffee, Zhao & Leshner, 1994). Many of them concentrate particularly on agenda setting effects (Behr & Iyengar, 1985; McCombs & Shaw, 1972). These analyses demonstrate

FIGURE 4. Structural Model of Voter Behavior II

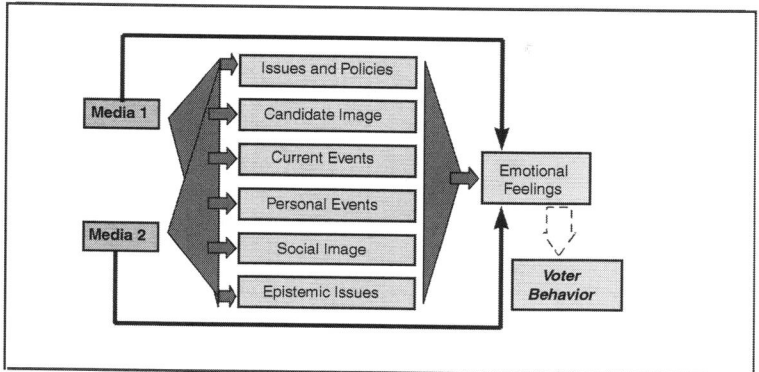

that the information policy of particular TV channels selects subjects on which voters' discussions as well as the attentions of political marketers concentrate (Newman, 1994; Perloff & Kinsey, 1992). On the other hand, social and political events have a feedback influence on the contents of the media's message. Besides, this message is often based (sometimes unconsciously) on preferences and political beliefs of the creators of information programs or owners of a given channel. Voters also add their own interpretations of the information they receive, depending on their knowledge or ideology–which can be identified with particular domains of the model.

Figure 5 presents this third hypothesis of mutual relations between the media, cognitive domains, emotional feelings and voter behavior.

METHOD

Subjects. The empirical research was conducted all over Poland in November 2000, a month after the Polish presidential election. Two hundred forty respondents were chosen randomly, taking into account demographic features. Men were 45% of the sample, women–54.17%.[1] As far as age is concerned, the 45% of the sample consisted of respondents between 18 and 29 years of age, 29.17% of the sample were between 30 and 44 years, and 25% of the sample were above the age of 44 years. Respondents with primary and vocational education were 12.92% of the sample, with secondary education–57.91%, and with

FIGURE 5. Structural Model of Voter Behavior III

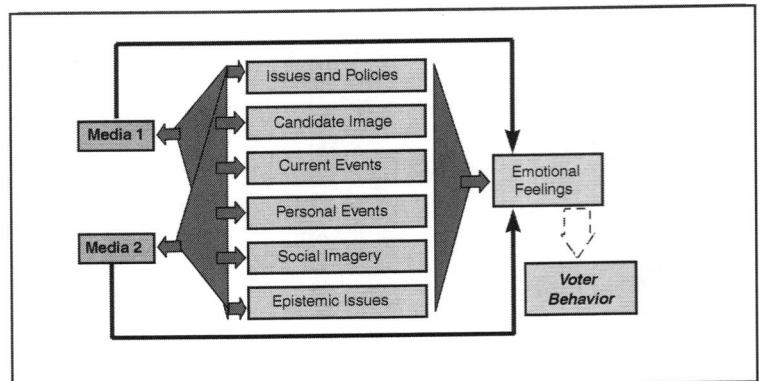

higher education– 27.92%. The majority of the respondents came from big cities (52.92%), whereas 31.67% came from small towns, and 14.58% from rural areas.

The questionnaire. The respondents filled out individually a questionnaire consisting of nine sections. Section I concerned political preferences. They were asked to specify which of the 12 candidates competing in the 2000 elections they were voting for; to give their preferences for Polish political parties; their level of interest in politics; their own political ideology.

Sections II to VII included questions connected with the seven domains specified in Newman and Sheth's model. Items in Section II: Issues and Policies asked the respondent to specify the views of the candidate the respondent was voting for on the economy, foreign affairs and domestic social issues. Section III: Social Imagery included questions on what support, according to the respondent, "his or her" candidate received in 19 various social groups (workmen, farmers, entrepreneurs, religious believers, women, men, etc.). Section IV: Candidate Image and Emotional Feelings consisted of three items. The first was connected with the respondent's opinion on whether the candidate he or she was voting for had one of the specified 16 features of character (e.g., honest, truthful, hard-working, sincere, decisive, etc.). The second question was a standard feeling thermometer on which the respondent marked his or her attitude to the preferred candidate on the scale from 0–"extremely negative feeling" to 100–"extremely positive feeling," where 50 represented "neutral feeling." The third item consisted of 14 bipolar 7-point adjective scales, which were used to evaluate the candidate's image (for a detailed description of the scales, see Cwalina, Falkowski & Kaid, 2000). Section V: Current Events was concerned with the respondent's attitude to ten possible events, which could change his or her voting decision. Section VI: Personal Events included ten possible pieces of information from the candidate's personal life that could change the respondent's voting decision. Section VII: Epistemic Issues refers to reasons that would justify the perceived satisfaction of curiosity, knowledge, and exploratory needs offered by the candidate.

Section VIII of the questionnaire referred to the media. The respondents expressed their own opinions on 5-point Likert scales on the influence of the media and opinion polls on voting decisions and democratic processes.

Finally, the respondents answered questions concerning such demographic variables as gender, age, education and place of residence.

RESULTS

During the first and the last balloting twelve candidates participated in the Polish presidential election. On the basis of the respondents' marked voting records, the research sample was divided into 12 electorates. There were only two candidates who were seriously considered in the election process: Aleksander Kwasniewski–the incumbent, and Andrzej Olechowski–the challenger. In the research sample Kwasniewski got 52.9% of votes while Olechowski got 34.5%. The official results of the Polish presidential election show that Kwasniewski obtained 54.5%, and Olechowski got 17.4%.

Therefore, in our analysis we have taken into account only the two dominant candidates, as only their sample research electorates are sufficiently large to enable us to perform statistical analysis. In the end data received from 208 respondents were analyzed, 126 of whom were supporters of Kwasniewski and 82 supporters of Olechowski.

Emotional Feelings as a Predictor Voter Behavior

Unfortunately, the data obtained do not allow us to determine directly the connection between emotional feelings measured by the feeling thermometer and the respondent's voting behavior because the respondents mentioned the candidate they were voting for and then, in the following parts of the questionnaire, they described their beliefs concerning only this particular candidate. Therefore, it is impossible to compare emotional feelings of the same respondent toward different candidates. However, based on the results of previous research on the power of this relationship, it is possible to conduct some indirect analyses on the collected data (see Table 1).

Among Kwasniewski's electorate the average temperature of feelings toward him was $M_K = 69.77$ ($\sigma_K = 14.64$), whereas among Olechowski's electorate–$M_O = 68.49$ ($\sigma_O = 17.71$). It can be assumed that for the whole population the average is $\mu = 50$, since the distribution of the temperature of feelings is a normal distribution and has no known standard deviation (Cwalina & Falkowski, 1999). Therefore, if the temperatures toward Kwasniewski and Olechowski are considerably higher from the average for the population, then it is legitimate to say that voters voted for a "warmer" candidate.

In order to verify this hypothesis, a test was conducted for the average in the population with unknown standard deviation based on Student's t-distribution (Blalock, 1960). Both in Kwasniewski's and Olechowski's case, the average temperatures of their supporters differed considerably from the average in the population: $t = 15.03$, $df = 124$, $p < .001$ and $t = 9.28$, $df = 79$, $p < .001$, respectively. Besides, the average of feelings toward these two candidates did not differ considerably from one another ($t = 0.56$, $df = 203$, $p = .58$).

Therefore, it can be assumed that the respondents actually vote for a candidate toward whom they have more positive emotional attitudes.

Media

In order to simplify the structure of data with reference to the importance of the media in forming voting preferences we conducted a principal component analysis on the items from the media section in the questionnaires separately for Kwasniewski's and Olechowski's electorates. We obtained two different factors for each of them (see Table 2).

Among Kwasniewski's electorate a two-factor solution was obtained, which account for 58.07% of the total variance. Factor 1 called "Media 1" refers to the media and polls in elections and explains 40.97% of the variance, whereas Factor 2 defined as "Media 2" may be defined as money and media in democracy (17.09%).

Among Olechowski's electorate two factors were also distinguished which accounting for 43.11% of the total variance. Factor 1 (Media 1)

TABLE 2. Results of Principal Component Analysis for Media

Aleksander Kwasniewski		Andrzej Olechowski	
Factor 1 *Media 1: Media and polls in election*	40.97%	**Factor 1** *Media 1: Polls and money in elections*	27.39%
I used information from the media to make my choice in this election.	.82	I used information from the polls to make my choice in this election.	.79
I used information from the polls to make my choice in this election.	.80	Polls serve a useful role in elections.	.76
Polls serve a useful role in elections.	.69	Money has influence on the media.	.54
The media serves a useful role in elections.	.56		
Factor 2 *Media 2: Money and media in democracy*	17.09%	**Factor 2** *Media 2: Media in elections and democracy*	15.72%
Money has influence on the media.	.74	I think that advertising strengthens democracy.	.67
I think that advertising strengthens democracy.	.71	The media serves a useful role in elections.	.64
I think that polling strengthens democracy.	.55	I used information from the media to make my choice in this election.	.49
		I think that polling strengthens democracy.	.48
Total variance accounted for:	58.07%		43.11%

refers to polls and money in election (27.39%), and Factor 2 (Media 2)–the media in elections and democracy (15.72%).

The above-mentioned factor solutions were used in testing individual structural equations models, depending on a given candidate's electorate.

Structural Equation Model I

In order to verify structural models a methodology based on the analysis of structural equations was used, defined also as path analysis (see Loehlin, 1987). It is a statistical method making it possible to verify hypotheses concerning the structure of causal dependencies in a defined set of variables.

Structural Equation Model I for Aleksander Kwasniewski

Figure 6 presents the empirical structural equation model I for Aleksander Kwasniewski. The arrows represent relevant statistical relations between particular elements of the model. A relevant statistically standardized parameter of the path was marked above each of them. The bold arrows represent a "complete" causal sequence, that is one starting from Media and finishing with Voter Behavior. The arrow

FIGURE 6. Empirical Structural Model of Voter Behavior I: *Aleksander Kwasniewski*

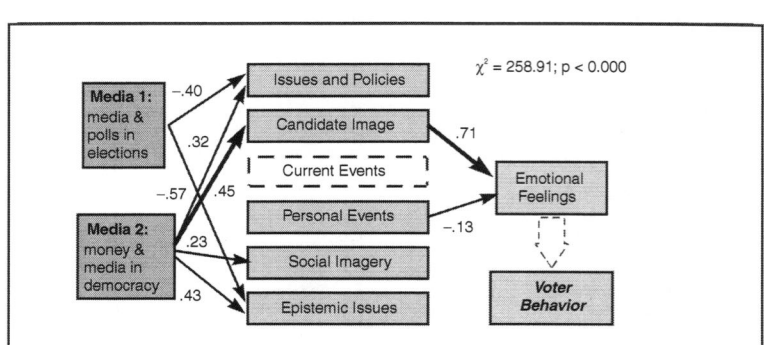

connecting Emotional Feelings with Voter Behavior represents a hypothetical established connection between these domains.

The structural solution presented in Figure 6 does not meet statistical requirements of goodness-of-fit ($\chi^2 = 258.91$, p < .001). Therefore, we have to reject model I for Kwasniewski as it doesn't fit the empirical data. However, some of the paths are significant. The cognitive domains which "warm up" the voters feeling toward Kwasniewski are: positive Candidate Image and lack of important Personal Events. The media significantly influence four domains: Issues and Policies, Social Imagery, Candidate Image, and Personal Events. Besides, there is only one "complete" causal sequence (bold arrows). The more the respondents recognize the importance of money and media in democracy, the more positive Kwasniewski's image seems to them. This, as a result, leads to an increase in emotional attitudes toward him and finally influences their voting behavior.

Structural Equation Model I for Andrzej Olechowski

A somewhat different picture emerges when we look at this same structural model concerning the Olechowski's electorate (see Figure 7).

This model also does not fit the empirical data ($\chi^2 = 123.25$, p < .001). Nevertheless it is worth noticing that the path structure differs from that of Kwasniewski's model. It seems that the media impact is lower than in model I for Kwasniewski as there are only three cognitive domains, Social Imagery, Candidate Image, and Epistemic Issues, that

FIGURE 7. Empirical Structural Model of Voter Behavior I: *Andrzej Olechowski*

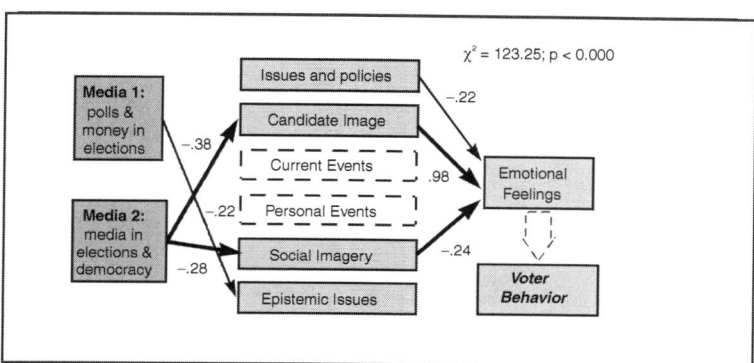

are significantly influenced by this factor. Emotional Feelings toward Olechowski depend on three domains: Issues and Policies, Social Imagery and Candidate Image. However, in the case of the two first domains, it is a negative relation (negative parameters of the path).

Two "complete" causal sequences were distinguished: Media 2: *Media in elections and democracy*–Candidate Image–Emotional Feelings, and Media 2–Social Imagery–Emotional Feelings. It is interesting to observe that if the respondents believe the media play a large role, it influences in a negative way both Olechowski's image and the perceived social support for him.

Structural Equation Model II

In the hypothetical structural model presented in Figure 4 two paths were added which directly connect the media with the thermometer feeling.

Structural Equation Model II for Aleksander Kwasniewski

The fit of the model to empirical data is better than in the previous Kwasniewski model, however, it is still very poor ($\chi^2 = 173.22$, p < .001). The path structure is presented in Figure 8.

The media influence most of the cognitive domains, but only Personal Events impact on emotional attitudes. The hypothetical, direct connections between the perception of the media's role and emotions toward Kwasniewski turned out to be statistically irrelevant; how-

FIGURE 8. Empirical Structural Model of Voter Behavior II: *Aleksander Kwasniewski*

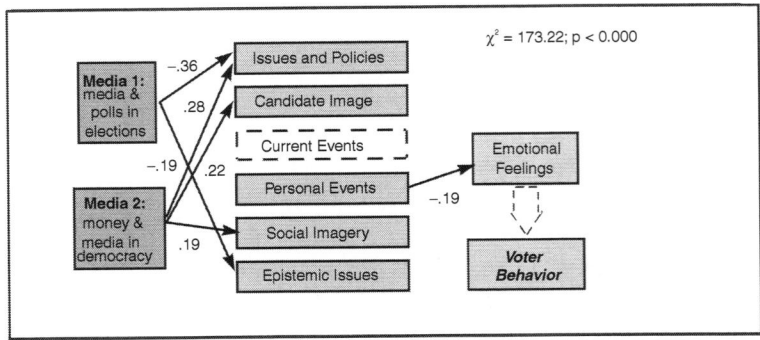

ever, adding them to the initial model II changed the structure of the paths in the empirical model II. No "complete" causal sequence occurred.

Structural Equation Model II for Andrzej Olechowski

The path structure for Olechowski also didn't change with reference to model I at all, except that the χ^2 is lower than in the first model ($\chi^2 = 115.52$, $p < .001$), but still its goodness-of-fit is very weak. Empirical model II for Olechowski is presented in Figure 9.

The significant paths are similar to the ones obtained in the case of the empirical model I for Olechowski. Also the "complete" causal sequences are connected with the same domains as in the previous case.

The better fits of the models II to the empirical data of Kwasniewski's and Olechowski's electorates show that the media's influence on emotional feelings toward the candidates does make sense. It is worthwhile remembering that "media" is understood here, as the voters' beliefs that media exert an influence on elections.

Structural Equation Model III

The last, third models assume the mutual relationship between the media and the six cognitive domains and all six domains plus media directly influence the thermometer. This hypothetical model is presented in Figure 5.

Structural Equation Model III for Aleksander Kwasniewski

The results of fitting model III to the empirical data of Kwasniewski's electorate are presented in Figure 10.

The model goodness-of-fit parameter ($\chi^2 = 30.37$, p < .001) allows us to treat this model as an adequate approximation of the empirical data. The model structure shows that only three paths are significant: Candidate Image and Current Events influence Media, and Personal Events

FIGURE 9. Empirical Structural Model of Voter Behavior II: *Andrzej Olechowski*

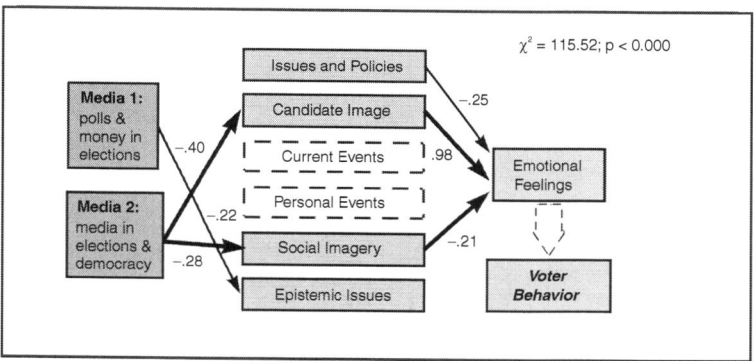

FIGURE 10. Empirical Structural Model of Voter Behavior III: *Aleksander Kwasniewski*

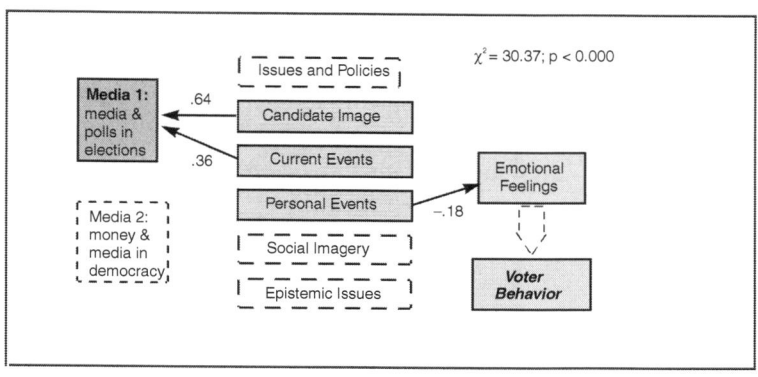

exert a negative impact on Emotional Feelings. No "complete" causal sequence was found in the above model.

Structural Equation Model III for Andrzej Olechowski

The empirical model III structure describing the Olechowski's electorate is much more complex (see Figure 11). The χ^2 coefficient ($\chi^2 = 19.10$, p < .005) is the lowest of all obtained, and even though it is not fully satisfactory, it allows us to treat this model as an adequate fit for the empirical data.

We see that the media influence some of the cognitive domains as much as the cognitive domains influence the media. Media 1: *Polls and money in elections* influence emotional attitude toward Olechowski. As in the case of model III for Kwasniewski, no "complete" causal sequence was found.

DISCUSSION AND PRACTICAL IMPLICATIONS

As the cognitive representations of voters differ across the two electorates, we can derive the following different conclusions and implications concerning the marketing strategy.

First of all, model III best fits the data of both Kwasniewski and Olechowski. The model structure is much more complex for Olechowski than for Kwasniewski, which means that emotional feelings toward

FIGURE 11. Empirical Structural Model of Voter Behavior III: *Andrzej Olechowski*

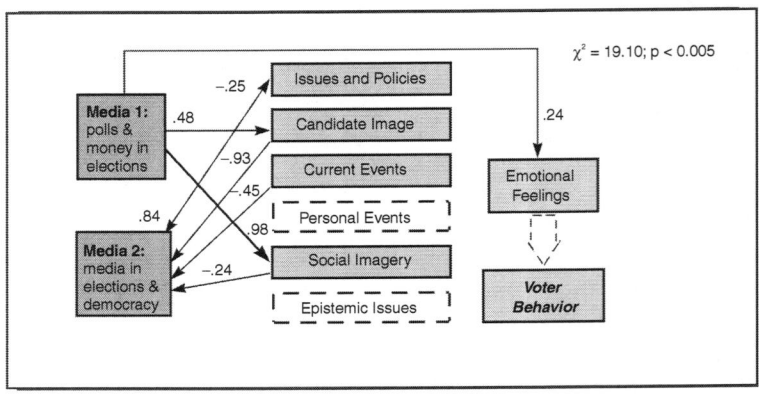

Olechowski are directly related to changes in the media and cognitive domains, and, thus, can be relatively easily controlled.

On the other hand, the model structure of Kwasniewski's electorate is less complex, which means that the voters' attitudes toward Kwasniewski are much more stable and solid. Changing the voters' beliefs in the cognitive domains does not change the emotional feelings toward Kwasniewski. However, one should take into account that Personal Events is an important cognitive domain, which impacts on emotional feelings. This significant path, which connects these two elements, is presented in all three tested models. That means that the most likely way to "warm up" or "cool down" the emotional feelings toward Kwasniewski would be to operate on Personal Events (see Table 3). How to do this is still a question, as we don't observe a significant connection between this cognitive domain and the media. One solution seems to be shifting the main emphasis in the electoral campaign to direct marketing (meetings with voters, activating volunteers, etc.).

The other interesting observation is so-called "underdog effect." This phenomenon describes the situation in which voters vote for that candidate, who has lower social support and lower standing in the polls. As the cognitive domain Social Imagery can be understood as the perceived range and amount of social support, the research results provide empirical support for this underdog effect. It can be best observed in models I and II for Olechowski in which we notice that Media 2: *Media in elections and democracy* influences significantly Social Imagery (see Figure 7 and 9). This means that if voters are more convinced that media influence the outcome of elections, they perceive lower social support for Olechowski. This is shown by the negative value of the path parameter. And, the lower this support, the "warmer" the candidate. In other words, decreasing Social Imagery increases emotional feelings.

TABLE 3. Personal Events

I'd change my vote if the candidate I supported:	
• Committed a serious crime.	• Cheated on his tax returns.
• Lied about events in his private life.	• Became too seriously ill to work effectively.
• Was involved in a business scandal.	• Had serious family trouble.
• Was involved in a political scandal.	• Was caught driving drunk.
• Changed his stand on the issues	• Was a communist secret services collaborator.

In the case of Kwasniewski's electorate, the Media 2: *Money and media in democracy* influences Social Imagery also, but in a positive way. However, there is no connection between this domain and emotional attitudes toward Kwasniewski.

The research presented here points to the important elements on which one must concentrate in order to conduct an effective electoral campaign. It also demonstrates that no universal ways of running such campaigns should be developed because different cognitive domains of different candidates are relevant for voting preferences. The promotional campaign of candidates for state offices should then be developed individually for each candidate. Such an individually developed strategy can be prepared on the basis of an analysis of cause-effect relations using the methodology of structural equations presented in this article.

NOTE

1. Percents do not add up to 100%, because not every respondent completed the section on demographic characteristics.

REFERENCES

Abelson, R.P., Kinder, D.R., Peters, M.D., & Fiske, S.T. (1982). Affective and semantic components in political person perception. *Journal of Personality and Social Psychology* 42: 619-630.

Ansolabehere, S., Iyengar, S., & Simon, A. (1995). Evolving perspectives on the effects of campaign communication. *Research in Political Sociology* 7: 13-31.

Aronson, E., Wilson, T.D., & Akert, R.M. (1994). *Social psychology: The heart and the mind.* New York: HarperCollins College Publishers.

Behr, R., & Iyengar, S. (1985). Television news, real-world cues and changes in the public agenda. *Public Opinion Quarterly* 58(4): 479-508.

Berelson, B., Lazarsfeld, P., & McPhee, W. (1954). *Voting: A study of opinion formation in a presidential campaign.* Chicago, IL: University Chicago of Press.

Blalock, H.M. (1960). *Social statistics.* New York: McGraw-Hill.

Campbell, A., Converse, P.E., Miller, W.E., & Stokes, D.E. (1960). *The American voter.* New York: John Wiley.

Chaffee, S.H., Zhao, X., & Leshner, G. (1994). Political knowledge and the campaign media of 1992. *Communication Research* 21(3): 305-324.

Converse, P.E. (1964). The nature of belief systems in mass public. In *Ideology and discontent*, edited by D.E. Apter (pp. 206-261). New York: The Free Press of Glencoe.

Cwalina, W., & Falkowski, A. (1999). Decision processes in perception in the political preferences research: A comparative analysis of Poland, France, and Germany. *Journal for Mental Changes* 5(2): 27-49.

Cwalina, W., & Falkowski, A. (2000). Psychological mechanisms of political persuasion: The influence of political advertising on voting behavior. *Polish Psychological Bulletin* 31(3): 203-222.

Cwalina, W., Falkowski, A., & Kaid, L.L. (2000). Role of advertising in forming the image of politicians: Comparative analysis of Poland, France, and Germany. *Media Psychology* 2(2): 119-146.

Cwalina, W., Falkowski, A., & Roznowski, B. (1999). Television spots in Polish presidential elections. In *Television and politics in evolving European democracies*, edited by L.L. Kaid (pp. 45-60). Commack, NY: Nova Science Publishers.

Dalton, R.J., & Wattenberg, M.P. (1993). The not so simple act of voting. In *The state of the discipline II*, edited by A. Finifter (pp. 193-218). Washington, DC: The American Political Science Association.

Downs, A. (1957). *A economic theory of democracy*. New York: Harper.

Falkowski, A., & Cwalina, W. (1999). Methodology of constructing effective political advertising. An empirical study of the Polish presidential election in 1995. In *Handbook of Political Marketing*, edited by B.I. Newman (pp. 283-304). Thousand Oaks, CA: Sage.

Harrison, M. (1965). Television and radio. In *The British general election of 1964*, edited by D. Butler & A. King (pp. 156-184). London: Macmillan.

Johnston, R.J., Pattie, C.J., & Allsopp, J.G. (1988). *A nation dividing? The electoral map of Great Britain 1979-1987*. London: Longman.

Kaid, L.L. (ed.). (1999). *Television and politics in evolving European democracies*. Commack, NY: Nova Science Publishers.

Loehlin, J.C. (1987). *Latent variable models: An introduction to factor, path, and structural analysis*. Hillsdale, NJ: Lawrence Erlbaum.

Lott, B., Lott, A., & Saris, R. (1993). Voter preference and behavior in the presidential election of 1988. *Journal of Psychology* 127(1): 87-97.

Masterson, J.T., & Biggers, T. (1986). Emotion-eliciting qualities of television campaign advertising as a predictor of voting behavior. *Psychology: A Quarterly Journal of Human Behavior* 23(1): 13-19.

McCombs, M., & Shaw, D.L. (1972). The agenda-setting function of mass media. *Public Opinion Quarterly* 36: 176-187.

Negrine, R. (1994). *Politics and the mass media in Britain*. London: Routlege.

Newman, B.I. (1994). *The marketing of the president: Political marketing as campaign strategy*. Thousand Oaks, CA: Sage.

Newman, B.I. (1999). A predictive model of voter behavior: The repositioning of Bill Clinton. In *Handbook of political marketing*, edited by B.I. Newman (pp. 259-282). Thousand Oaks, CA: Sage.

Newman, B.I., & Sheth, J.N. (1985). A model of primary voter behavior. *Journal of Consumer Research* 12: 178-187.

Page, B.I. (1977). Elections and social choice: The state of the evidence. *American Journal of Political Science* 21(3): 639-668.

Perloff, R.M., & Kinsey, D. (1992). Political advertising as seen by consultants and journalists. *Journal of Advertising Research* 32(3): 53-60.

Popkin, S. (1991). *The reasoning voter: Communication and persuasion in presidential campaigns.* Chicago: University of Chicago Press.

Riley, M. (1988). *Power, politics, and voting behaviour: An introduction to the sociology of politics.* London: Harvester-Wheatsheaf.

Singh, K., Leong, S.M., Tan, C.T., & Wang, K.C. (1995). A theory of reasoned action perspective of voting behavior: Model and empirical test. *Psychology and Marketing* 12(1): 37-51.

Verčič, D. (1999). The politics of total communication. *Journal for Mental Changes*, 5(2): 51-63.

Testing a Predictive Model
of Voter Behavior
on the 2000 U.S. Presidential Election

Bruce I. Newman

DePaul University, USA

SUMMARY. Utilizing a predictive model of voter behavior, this study identified the motivations behind a sample of voters who cast a ballot for George W. Bush and Al Gore in the 2000 presidential campaign. The motivations of the voters were differentiated on the basis of the "value" they sought in a president. In other words, just as companies in the "commercial marketplace" have to create value to attract customers, so does a candidate in the "political marketplace" who is seeking to carve out a niche for himself that separates him from his competition. Pairwise discriminant analysis is used to identify the motivations behind the choice behavior of voters at both the candidate and party level. The results reveal the complimentary roles that the political party and each candidate's campaign organization played in their respective marketing strategies. *[Article copies available for a fee from The Haworth Document Delivery Service: 1-800-HAWORTH. E-mail address: <getinfo@haworthpressinc.*

Bruce I. Newman is Professor of Marketing in the Kellstadt Graduate School of Business at DePaul University, Department of Marketing, 1 East Jackson Boulevard, Chicago, IL 60604 USA (E-mail: bnewman@depaul.edu). He is also Editor of the *Journal of Political Marketing.*

[Haworth co-indexing entry note]: "Testing a Predictive Model of Voter Behavior on the 2000 U.S. Presidential Election." Newman, Bruce I. Co-published simultaneously in *Journal of Political Marketing* (The Haworth Political Press, an imprint of The Haworth Press, Inc.) Vol. 1, No. 2/3, 2002, pp. 159-173; and: *Communication of Politics: Cross-Cultural Theory Building in the Practice of Public Relations and Political Marketing* (eds: Bruce I. Newman, and Dejan Verčič) The Haworth Political Press, an imprint of The Haworth Press, Inc., 2002, pp. 159-173. Single or multiple copies of this article are available for a fee from The Haworth Document Delivery Service [1-800-HAWORTH, 9:00 a.m. - 5:00 p.m. (EST). E-mail address: getinfo@haworthpressinc.com].

10.1300/J199v01n02_11

KEYWORDS. Voter behavior, politcal marketing, U.S. presidential elections, candidate, political party

INTRODUCTION

The 2000 U.S. presidential election was used to test a predictive model of voter behavior in an effort to ascertain the motivations behind the choice behavior of voters who cast a ballot for Gore and Bush (Newman, 1999a).[1] To win this election, both Al Gore and George W. Bush had to position themselves in the minds of American voters that allowed them to attract the greatest number of voters. What is perhaps the greatest irony of all in this election was that the candidate who received the greatest number of votes in fact lost because of a complicated set of rules that exists in the United States. Still, the goal behind the marketing strategy of both candidates was to develop an image and campaign platform that would insure victory.

An important part of any political campaign is the candidates' spending of money and time to promote their ideas (Newman, 1994; Newman and Sheth, 1985a) and manufacture their image (Newman, 1999b, 2001a, 2001b). Thus, it has become important to understand why voters behave the way they do in addition to conducting polls that indicate who is going to vote for whom and by what margin one candidate will win or lose an election. By understanding why voters value one candidate over another, their behavior can be better understood, which will enable campaign organizations to spend their time and money wisely.

BACKGROUND

The same principles that operate in the commercial marketplace hold true in the political marketplace: Successful organizations, whether they are run by a corporation, political party, candidate, or interest group must have a market orientation and be constantly engaged in creating value for their customers. In other words, marketers must anticipate their customers' needs, and then constantly develop innovative products and services to keep their customers satisfied. Politicians have a similar orientation and are constantly trying to create value for voters by offering them the most benefit at the smallest cost (Kotler and Kotler, 1981).

A market orientation then requires that research and polling be done to help shape the policies of the politician, eventually becoming a campaign platform that is offered to the voter in exchange for his/her vote (Kotler and Kotler, 1999; Sherman, 1999). The use of marketing research, polling and focus groups to develop marketing strategies is now a well-accepted practice in politics (Mitofsky, 1998; Asher, 1998; Mitchell and Daves, 1999).

A marketing strategy is a plan of action that is used to implement a series of activities that will insure success in the marketplace. Once a candidate has been recruited, the role of a marketing strategy is to reinforce the candidate's "image" in the minds of the constituencies that will affect his/her success in the political marketplace. An image is created through the use of visual impressions that are communicated by the candidate's physical presence, media appearances, and experiences and record as a political leader as that information is integrated in the minds of citizens (Nimmo & Rivers, 1981; Schweiger & Adami, 1999; Baines, 1999). The position of the candidate is based on his image and the platform that is developed (O'Shaughnessy, 1990; Morris, 1997; Sherman, 1999; Kraus, 1999; Newman, 1999b). At the heart of that strategy will be the use of political advertising to reinforce the image in the minds of the voters (Kaid, 1981; Arterton, 1984; Kaid, 1999; Perloff, 1999).

Once a candidate wins the election, it is delivery time, a time when voters look to the president to carry out his promises (McGinnis, 1969; Nimmo, 1970; Maarek, 1995; Nimmo, 1996; O'Shaughnessy, 1990; Nimmo, 1999). Today, the modern day president must rely on marketing strategies developed by their team of consultants not only to win the election, but to be successful as a leader after entering the White House (Sabato, 1981; Jamieson, 1992; Wring, 1999; and Butler & Collins, 1999; Perloff, 1999; Johnson, 1999, 2001).

A MODEL OF VOTER BEHAVIOR

A model of voter behavior developed by Newman (1981) and tested by Newman (1999a) and Newman and Sheth (1985b, 1987) proposes a number of cognitive beliefs that may come from a wide range of sources, including the voter, word-of-mouth communication, and the mass media. In addition, the model incorporates the influence of an individual's affiliation with groups of people in his/her social environment (Lazarsfeld, Berelson, and Gaudet, 1944); and the influence of party affiliation and past voting behavior (Campbell et al., 1960). This model was used as the basis for the conduct of this study (see Figure 1).

The fundamental axiom of the model is that a voter is a consumer of a service offered by a politician, and similar to consumers in the commercial marketplace, voters choose candidates based on the perceived value they offer them. The model proposes that there are five distinct and separate cognitive domains that drive the voter's behavior. A key proposition of the model is that voter behavior can be driven by a combination of one or more of the domains in a given election. The model includes the following components:

Political Issues: This cognitive domain incorporates the policies a candidate advocates and promises to enact if elected to office, and is measured on a profile of benefits that the candidate advances in his platform. The formal definition is: "Political Issues refers to the personal beliefs of the voter about the candidate's stand on economic, social, and foreign policy issues, which represents the rationale for the candidate's platform" (Newman and Sheth, 1987, p. 31).

FIGURE 1. Model of Voter Behavior

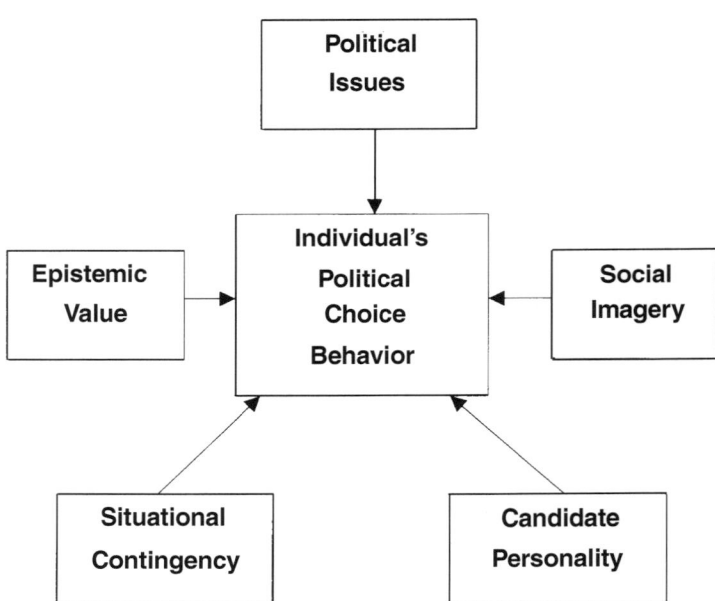

Social Imagery: This cognitive domain represents the stereotyping of the candidate to appeal to voters by making associations between the candidate and selected segments in society. This dimension is measured on a profile of stereotypes that represent one or more types of groups. The formal definition is: "Social Imagery refers to a candidate's image based on his association with specific demographic (age, sex), socio-economic (income, occupation), cultural-ethnic (Education, race), or political-ideological (conservative, moderate, liberal) segments of the society" (Newman and Sheth, 1987, p. 33).

Candidate Personality: This cognitive domain also represents the use of imagery in a slightly different way. Here, the candidate is emphasizing his personality traits to help reinforce and manufacture an image in the voters mind. This dimension is measured on a profile of personality traits representing one or more dimensions of the candidate's image. The formal definition is: "Candidate Personality refers to the emotional feelings such as hope, anger, patriotism, and pessimism aroused by the candidate's personality" (Newman and Sheth, 1987, p. 34).

Situational Contingency: This cognitive domain represents that dimension of voters thinking which could be swayed by "hypothetical events" described during the course of the campaign that they are led to believe could happen. This dimension is measured on a profile of situational contingencies representing one or more events that are likely to impact on the candidate. The formal definition is: "Situational contingency refers to a set of international, domestic, and/or personal events (contingencies) that might cause the voter to switch his vote to another candidate" (Newman and Sheth, 1987, p. 35).

Epistemic Value: This cognitive domain represents that dimension which appeals to a voter's sense of curiosity or novelty in choosing a candidate. This dimension is measured on a profile of curiosity issues. The formal definition is: "Epistemic value refers to the change of pace value a candidate acquires as a result of novelty, curiosity, boredom, or satiation associated with the election process" (Newman and Sheth, 1987, p. 36).

OVERVIEW OF THE STUDY

Setting

The study was carried out approximately 2 weeks before the presidential election in Chicago, Illinois. Respondents were asked to fill out

a survey before they voted, and to indicate their intention on the questionnaire. Information from the questionnaire was then used to carry out
the data analysis.

Sample

The study was carried out on 151 students, faculty and staff at DePaul
University. The sample included a slightly younger, better educated
sample of voters then one would find in the population as a whole. Approximately two-thirds of voters in both the Republican and Democratic parties were loyal to their party. Whereas close to 45% of the
voters were very interested in the results of the election, only 2% were
concerned about the outcome. This last statistic indicates that this was
an election that was not very exciting for voters, something that will be
revealed in the data analysis that follows (see Table 1).

Questionnaire Design

The questionnaire included statements that were operationalized
along the lines of each of the components in the predictive model of
voter behavior outlined in Figure 1. Measurement of the 5 values were
carried out using the following generic format:

1. Political Issues: Example: My candidate will be the best person
   to: Reduce the unemployment rate–Measured on a binary scale:
   Agree/Disagree.
2. Social Imagery: My candidate is the best person to help and will
   likely be supported by: Example: Blue collar workers–Measured
   on a binary scale: Most Likely/Least Likely.
3. Candidate Personality: I believe my candidate is: Example:
   Honest–Measured on a binary scale: Yes/No.
4. Situational Contingency: I would vote for another candidate if:
   Example: Prices and interest rates rose because of inflation–
   Measured on a binary scale: Yes/No.
5. Epistemic Value: I am voting for my candidate because: Example:
   I want a change in the administration–Measured on a binary scale:
   Yes/No.

Additionally, there were questions that dealt with voters' perceptions
concerning polls, media, money and other related issues to the election.

TABLE 1. General Profile of Sample Election: 2000 U.S. Presidential Campaign–Chicago

STUDY TIMING: APPROXIMATELY 2 WEEKS BEFORE ELECTION

SAMPLE SIZE: 15 USABLE SURVEYS–MAINLY DEPAUL UNIVERSITY STUDENTS AND FACULTY; SOME STAFF

AGE OF SAMPLE: 40% (18-30)

22% (31-45)

32% (46-64)

6% (65+)

EDUCATION OF SAMPLE: 13% HIGH SCHOOL DEGREE OR LESS

33% SOME COLLEGE

28% COLLEGE DEGREE

18% MASTERS OR DOCTORATE

8% PROFESSIONAL DEGREE

SOCIAL CLASS OF SAMPLE: 2% BELOW POVERTY LEVEL

9% LOWER MIDDLE CLASS

42% MIDDLE CLASS

38% UPPER MIDDLE CLASS

7% WEALTHY

2% OTHER

QUESTIONNAIRE: APPROXIMATELY 330 QUESTIONS–

1/2– ABOUT CANDIDATE CHOICE

1/2–ABOUT PARTY CHOICE

CANDIDATE PREFERENCE: 66—GEORGE W. BUSH

82—AL GORE

3—OTHER

PARTY LOYALTY: 20% OF BUSH SUPPORTERS MEMBERS OF PARTY

66% OF BUSH SUPPORTERS VOTED REPUBLICAN IN LAST ELECTION

31% OF GORE SUPPORTERS MEMBERS OF PARTY

73% OF GORE SUPPORTERS VOTED DEMOCRATIC IN LAST ELECTION

LEVEL OF INTEREST/CONCERN IN ELECTION:

43% OF BUSH SUPPORTERS VERY INTERESTED

45% OF GORE SUPPORTERS VERY INTERESTED

2% OF TOTAL SAMPLE VERY CONCERNED ABOUT ELECTION RESULTS

A total of 330 questions were included in the survey. Of the total number of questions, approximately one-half dealt with the candidates and one-half dealt with the parties. Each of the components in the model were modified slightly to orient the questions towards the political party of each candidate (Democrats-Gore; Republicans-Bush).

Data Analysis

The principal statistical technique used to carry out the data analysis was discriminant analysis.[2] Two sets of pairwise discriminant analyses were carried out between respondents who indicated that they preferred each candidate (George W. Bush and Al Gore) and preferred each party (Republican and Democrat). In these analyses, the criterion variable was the respondent's preferred candidate and party they belonged to. The predictor variables were questions generated for each of the components in the theory using a series of pairwise T-tests between respondent groups (e.g., Gore versus Bush supporters and Democrats versus Republicans). The procedural details and the mathematical theory underlying discriminant analysis is found in several books.[3]

DISCUSSION

The data results in Table 2 report on the discriminant analysis carried out between voters who identified themselves as either Republicans or Democrats. The four most important values to voters who identified themselves as Republicans were, in order of importance:

1. Gun control;
2. Desire for change in the administration;
3. Low inflation; and
4. My party supports patriotic candidates.

A review of these top four issues suggests that the Republican Party was successful in positioning itself as a party that would respond to two key issues, gun control and low inflation. Both of these issues have historically been important to this party. What is not surprising is the strong desire for change in the administration, as these are voters who

TABLE 2. Discriminant Analysis Results for Party Supporters: Four Most Important Variables Listed for Each Party

A. **Republican Party**

1. My support for presidential candidates and political parties depends on their position on gun control (discriminant coefficient = $-.49$).

2. I am supporting my political party because I want a change in the administration (discriminant coefficient = $-.46$).

3. I believe the party I support will keep inflation low (discriminant coefficient = $-.44$).

4. I believe my party only supports candidates who are patriotic (discriminant coefficient = $-.39$).

B. **Democratic Party**

1. My party is the best party to help and will likely be supported by the poor ($15,000 a year or less) (discriminant coefficient = .78).

2. I believe the party I support will assure women's equity in the job market (discriminant coefficient = .49).

3. My party is the best party to help and will likely be supported by blue collar workers (discriminant coefficient = .30).

4. My party is the best party to help and will likely by supported by unions (discriminant coefficient = .23).

Group Means: Republican = -3.12
Democratic = -1.79

Eigenvalue	Wilks' lambda	chi-squared	df	significance
5.73	.14	144.98	30	.00

Classification analysis

		Predicted		
Actual	Rep	Dem		Subjects
Rep.	33	1		34
Dem.	0	59		59

Correctly classified: 98.9%

had seen the democrats in the White House for the past 8 years. The last issue dealt with the perception of the Republican Party as one that supports patriotic candidates, a very key component to George W. Bush's campaign in 2000. The discriminant model predicted respondents' voter behavior with an astonishing 98.9% level of accuracy, an indication that the predictive model of voter behavior worked quite well at the party level.

The four most important values to voters who identified themselves as Democrats were, in order of importance:

1. Support of the democratic party by the poor;
2. The issue of women's equity in the job market;
3. Support of the democratic party by blue collar workers; and
4. Support of the democratic party by the unions.

An examination of this data suggests that the democrats were able to successfully target their cause to the stronghold of their party, namely unions, blue collar workers and the poor. In addition, they appealed to women voters with a promise to fight for their equity in the marketplace. Whereas this clearly explains the strong support that the democrats received from voters in 2000, it does bring to light the problem of the party, and that is their ability to reach out to voters who don't fit the classic democratic profile. Bill Clinton was able to market himself to a group of voters in both 1992 and 1996 that were not only your traditional blue collar, union workers, and it was that appeal that enabled Clinton to win the White House.

The data results in Table 3 report on the discriminant analysis carried out between voters who identified themselves as either Bush or Gore supporters. Specifically, these respondents indicated a likelihood that they would vote for each of these candidates in the upcoming Presidential election. The four most important values to voters who identified themselves as Bush supporters were, in order of importance:

1. Desire for a change in the administration;
2. Support by middle-aged adults;
3. Support by white collar workers; and
4. Support by executives.

An examination of these results reveals a preference for George W. Bush first of all because he presented to voters a change from the "Clinton-tainted" Gore who reminded the country of all the troubles associated with the tenure of President Clinton. But a key base of support for Bush came because of the perception that he was aligned in people's minds by the traditional base of Republican voters, namely white collar workers and executives. The support from middle-aged adults came as a result of the issues that Bush advocated in his platform, primarily his promise to offer a tax cut to the American people, an issue that would clearly resonate with voters in this age category.

TABLE 3. Discriminant Analysis Results for Candidate Supporters: Four Most Important Variables Listed for Each Candidate

A. **George W. Bush**

1. I am voting for my candidate because I want a change in the administration (discriminant coefficient = −.69).

2. My candidate is the best person to help and will likely be supported by middle aged adults (46-64) (discriminant coefficient = −.42).

3. My candidate is the best person to help and will likely be supported by white collar workers (discriminant coefficient = −.24).

4. My candidate is the best person to help and will likely be supported by executives (CEOs, COOs, CFOs) (discriminant coefficient = −.19).

B. **Al Gore**

1. My candidate is the best party to help and will likely be supported by the poor ($15,000 a year or less) (discriminant coefficient = .42).

2. My candidate will be the best person to reduce the unemployment rate (discriminant coefficient = .31).

3. My candidate will be the best person to initiate a broad-based healthcare program (discriminant coefficient = .16).

4. My candidate will be the best person to plan affordable housing for young families (discriminant coefficient = .14).

Group Means: Bush = −2.52
Gore = 1.94

Eigenvalue	Wilks' lambda	chi-squared	df	significance
5.03	.16	136.56	28	.00

Classification analysis

		Predicted		
Actual	Bush	Gore	Subjects	
Bush	40	0	40	
Gore	2	50	52	

Correctly classified: 97.8%

The four most important values to Gore supporters were:

1. Support from the poor;
2. Will reduce unemployment;
3. Will initiate a broad-based healthcare program; and
4. Will plan affordable housing for young families.

The support generated by Gore, on the other hand, was connected to the issues that he advocated so strongly, namely healthcare, housing and unemployment. Along with the issues was the strong link that Gore made between his programs and the poor. The strong support of Gore because of the issues reveals a dimension of his strategy that could have been improved upon, namely, his personal appeal to voters on an emotional level.

This discriminant model predicted with 97.8% accuracy, indicating that it worked equally as well at the party as well as candidate level.

CONCLUSION

This study reported on the application of a predictive model of voter behavior that was used in the 2000 U.S. Presidential election. The study reported in this paper led to the conclusion that voters choose a president primarily on the basis of who the candidate is and what he stands for, and secondarily, on the basis of his connection to a political party. Through the use of discriminant analysis, the model proved to be a very viable tool to use to test voter choice behavior at both the candidate and party level, as classification results were reported in the high 90th percentile for both models (see Tables 2 and 3).

Beyond the use of the predictive model of voter behavior as a tool to analyze voter behavior in democracies where voter choice may be based on either a candidate or party basis, the model is invaluable in reporting the specific appeals that proved to be most effective for both the candidates and parties in their attempt to win over voters in the Presidential campaign (Newman, 1999a). The data results reported support some rather traditional models of party support for both the democrats and republicans, as each one targets issues that have very different levels of appeal to each party.

What proved to be a very revealing insight into the election, however, was the strong desire for change at both the party and candidate level for Mr. Bush, and the rather unemotional support that Mr. Gore received from his supporters. Mr. Gore ran a strong issues-oriented campaign, and this was supported by the results of the discriminant model reported in Table 3.

Mr. Bush on the other hand ran a campaign that was short on details (as reflected in the lack of issues that were identified in the discriminant model at the candidate level–Table 3) but with an emphasis on his ability to bring change to Washington D.C. (as reflected by the desire for change in the administration that came out in both the party and candidate discriminant models).

What turned out to be most effective for Mr. Bush as one looks at the election results in hindsight but in conjunction with the results presented in this paper was his ability to have the party speak to issues as he spoke on a broader level to the American voters about the change he would bring to the White House.

As democracies continue to evolve around the world, the model reported in this paper will be a very useful tool to examine the comparative role and influence that both the candidate and party play in winning over voters.

NOTES

1. The author would like to thank Judith Ross of DePaul University for her help in collecting the data for this study.

2. Discriminant analysis is ideally suited to the model's operationalization because discriminant analysis begins with known groups, such as voters. In applying the model, the objective is to classify these known groups on the basis of values driving choice, namely each component in the predictive model of voter behavior. Discriminant analysis accomplishes this by maximizing between-group variance and minimizing within-group variance to create mutually exclusive and collectively exhaustive groups. Once the groups have been distinguished, discriminant analysis allows the researcher to determine which variables account for the greatest discrimination. Those values that discriminate significantly are associated with large coefficients, resulting in implications to strategy development. The predictive power associated with a discriminant model can be evaluated by comparing the predicted versus the actual group memberships, as identified in the questionnaire. Classification analysis thus provides an indication of the model's predictive validity.

3. Haire, Mason. "Projective Techniques in Marketing Research." *Journal of Marketing* 14 (April 1950): 649-656; Jackson, Barbara Bund. *Multivariate Data Analysis: An Introduction.* Homewood, Ill.: Richard D. Irwin, 1983; Klecka, William R. *Discriminant Analysis.* Newbury Park, Calif.: Sage Publications, 1980.

REFERENCES

Arterton, F. Christopher. (1984). *Media Politics: The News Strategies of Presidential Campaigns.* Lexington, MA: Lexington Books.

Asher, H. (1998). *Polling and the Public: What Every Citizen Should Know* (4th ed.). Washington, DC: Congressional Quarterly Press.

Asher, H. (1992). *Polling and the Public,* Washington, DC, Congressional Quarterly Press, p. 96.

Asher, H. B. (1998). *Polling and the Public: What Every Citizen Should Know* (4th ed.). Washington, DC: Congressional Quarterly Press.

Baines, P. (1999). Voter segmentation and candidate positioning. In B. I. Newman (Ed.). *Handbook of political marketing*. 403-420. Thousand Oaks, CA: Sage.

Butler, P. and Collins, N. (1999). A conceptual framework for political marketing. In B. I. Newman (Ed.), *Handbook of political marketing*. 55-72. Thousand Oaks, CA: Sage.

Campbell, Angus et al. (1960). *The American Voter*. New York: John Wiley and Sons.

Goldenberg, E. N., & Traugott, M. W. (1984). *Campaigning for Congress*. Washington, DC: Congressional Quarterly Press.

Greenfield, J.(1982). *The Real Campaign: How the Media Missed the Story of the 1980 Campaign*. New York: Summit Books.

Jamieson, K. H. (1992). *Dirty Politics: Deception, Distraction, and Democracy*. New York: Oxford University Press.

Johnson, D. W. (1999). The cyberspace election of the future. In B. I. Newman (Ed.), *Handbook of political marketing*. 705-724. Thousand Oaks, CA: Sage.

Johnson, D. W. (2001). *No Place for Amateurs: How Political Consultants Are Reshaping American Democracy*. London: Routledge.

Kaid, L. L. (1981). Political advertising. In D. D. Nimmo & K. R. Sanders (Eds.), *Handbook of political communication*. 249-271. Beverly Hills, CA: Sage.

Kaid, L. L. (1999). Political advertising: A summary of research findings. In B. I. Newman (Ed.), *Handbook of political marketing*. 423-438. Thousand Oaks, CA: Sage.

Kotler, P. & Kotler, N. (1981). Business Marketing for Political Candidates. *Campaigns and Elections*, 2, 24-33.

Kotler, P. & Kotler, N. (1999). Political marketing: Generating effective candidates, campaigns, and causes. In B. I. Newman (Ed.), *Handbook of political marketing*. 3-18. Thousand Oaks, CA: Sage.

Kraus, S. (1999). Televised debates: Marketing presidential candidates. In B. I. Newman (Ed.), *Handbook of political marketing*. 389-402. Thousand Oaks, CA: Sage.

Lazarsfeld, Paul, Bernard Berelson, & Hazel Gaudet. (1944). *The People's Choice: How the Voter Makes Up His Mind in a Presidential Campaign*. New York: Columbia University Press.

Maarek, P. J. (1995). *Political Marketing and Communication*. London: John Libby.

McGinnis, J. (1969). *The Selling of the President 1968*. New York: Trident.

Mitchell, P. & Daves, R. (1999). Media polls, candidates, and campaigns. In B. I. Newman (Ed.), *Handbook of political marketing*. 177-196. Thousand Oaks, CA: Sage.

Mitofsky, W. (1998). Was 1996 a worse year for polls than 1948? *Public Opinion Quarterly*, 62, 230-249.

Morris, D. (1997). *Behind the Oval Office*. New York: Random House.

Newman, B. I. (2001a). An Assessment of the 2000 U.S. Presidential Election: A Set of Political Marketing Guidelines. *Journal of Public Affairs* (pp. 210-216), Vol. 1, No. 3.

Newman, B. I. (2001b). The Role of Political Marketing in the United States. *European Journal of Marketing* (pp. 966-970), Vol. 35, No. 9/10.

Newman, Bruce I. (1999a). A predictive model of voter behavior: The repositioning of Bill Clinton. In (Ed.). B. I. Newman. *Handbook of political marketing* (pp. 259-282). Thousand Oaks, CA: Sage Publications.

Newman, Bruce I. (1999b). *The Mass Marketing of Politics: Democracy in an Age of Manufactured Images.* Thousand Oaks, CA: Sage Publications.

Newman, Bruce I. (1994). *The Marketing of the President: Political Marketing as Campaign Strategy.* Thousand Oaks, CA: Sage Publications.

Newman, Bruce I. and Jagdish N. Sheth. (1987). A *Theory of Political Choice Behavior.* New York: Praeger Publishers.

Newman, Bruce I., and Jagdish N. Sheth. (1985a). *Political Marketing: Readings and Annotated Bibliography.* Chicago: American Marketing Association.

Newman, Bruce I., and Jagdish N. Sheth. (1985b). A Model of Primary Voter Behavior. *Journal of Consumer Research,* 12, No.2, pp. 178-187.

Newman, B. I. (1981). The Prediction and Explanation of Actual Voting Behavior in a Presidential Primary Election. Unpublished doctoral dissertation, University of Illinois at Urbana-Champaign.

Nimmo, D. (1970). *The Political Persuaders.* Englewood Cliffs, NJ: Prentice Hall.

Nimmo D. (1996). Politics, media and modern democracy: The United States. In D. Swanson & P. Mancini (Eds.), *Politics, media, and modern democracy.* 29-47. Westport, CT: Praeger.

Nimmo, D. (1999). The permanent campaign: Marketing as a governing tool. In B. I. Newman (Ed.), *Handbook of political marketing.* 73-88. Thousand Oaks, CA: Sage.

O'Shaughnessy, N. J. (1990). *The Phenomenon of Political Marketing.* London: Macmillan.

O'Shaughnessy, N. J. (1999). Political marketing and political propaganda. In B. I. Newman (Ed.), *Handbook of political marketing.* 725-740. Thousand Oaks, CA: Sage.

Perloff, R. M. (1999). Elite, popular, and merchandised politics: Historical origins of presidential campaign marketing. In B.I. Newman (Ed.), *Handbook of political marketing.* 19-40. Thousand Oaks, CA: Sage.

Polsby, N. W. & Wildavsky, A. (1984). *Presidential Elections: Strategies of American Electoral Politics.* New York: Scribner.

Schweiger, Gunter and Michaela Adami. (1999). The nonverbal image of politicians and political parties. In B. I. Newman (Ed.), *Handbook of political marketing.* 347-364. Thousand Oaks, CA: Sage.

Sherman, E. (1999). Direct marketing: How does it work for political campaigns? In B. I. Newman (Ed.), *Handbook of political marketing.* 365-388. Thousand Oaks, CA: Sage.

Young, H. P. (1978). The Allocation of Funds in Lobbying and Campaigning. *Behavioral Science.* 23, 21-31.

Index

An environmentally friendly book printed and bound in England by www.printondemand-worldwide.com

PEFC Certified

This product is
from sustainably
managed forests
and controlled
sources

www.pefc.org

PEFC/16-33-415

MIX
Paper from
responsible sources
FSC® C004959

This book is made entirely of sustainable materials; FSC paper for the cover and PEFC paper for the text pages.

#0255 - 130514 - C0 - 212/152/10 - PB